A BIRDKEEPER

H Adams

PARAKEETS

A practical guide to keeping and breeding a wide range
of colourful parakeets from around the world

David Alderton

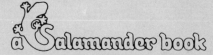
a Salamander book

Published by Salamander Books Limited
LONDON • NEW YORK

A Salamander Book

© 1989 Salamander Books Ltd.,
52 Bedford Row,
London WC1R 4LR,
United Kingdom.

ISBN 0 86101 437 5

Distributed in the UK by Hodder and Stoughton Services,
P.O.Box 6, Mill Road, Dunton Green, Sevenoaks, Kent TN13 2XX

All correspondence concerning the content of this volume
should be addressed to Salamander Books Ltd.

Author

David Alderton has kept and bred a wide variety of birds for twenty five
years. He has travelled extensively in pursuit of this interest, visiting
other enthusiasts in various parts of the world, including the United
States, Canada and Australia. He has previously written a number of
books on avicultural subjects, and contributes regularly to general and
specialist publications in the UK and overseas. David studied veterinary
medicine at Cambridge University, and now, in addition to writing,
runs a highly respected international service that offers advice on the
needs of animals kept in both domestic and commercial environments.
He is also a Council Member of the Avicultural Society.

Photographer

Cyril Laubscher has been interested in aviculture and ornithology for
more than thirty years and has travelled extensively in Europe,
Australia and Southern Africa photographing wildlife. When he left
England for Australia in 1966 as an enthusiastic aviculturalist,
this fascination found expression as he began to portray birds
photographically. In Australia he met the well-known aviculturalist
Stan Sindel and, as a result of this association, seventeen of Cyril's
photographs were published in Joseph Forshaw's original book on
Australian Parrots in 1969. Since then, his photographs have met with
considerable acclaim and the majority of those that appear here
were taken specially for this book.

Credits

Editor: Anne McDowall
Design: Jill Coote and Stonecastle Graphics
Colour reproductions: Bantam Litho Ltd.
Filmset: Gee Graphics
Printed in Belgium by Proost International Book Production

Contents

Above: *A pair of Sierra Parakeets*
Overleaf: *Pastel blue and sea green mutations of the Splendid Parakeet*

Introduction

There is no strict zoological distinction between parakeets and other parrots; 'parakeet' is simply the name used to describe parrots with long tails. The parakeet 'group' includes some of the most colourful and attractive members of the parrot family, many of which have been favourite aviary subjects for centuries (both the ancient Greeks and Romans kept parakeets). These birds continue to grow in popularity, both as pets and as aviary subjects, and a number of species are now well established, having bred successfully in captivity for many generations.

Parakeets, like other members of the parrot family, are widely distributed throughout the tropical and sub-tropical regions of the world. Australian species have proved the easiest to maintain and breed in European and North American collections, being relatively quiet and, in most cases, not especially destructive. The number of colour

mutations that have arisen in the more free-breeding species have created further interest in this group. Colour forms of the Ring-necked Parakeet are also well established, and new varieties are being developed. The members of this mainly Asiatic group, often known as the psittaculid parakeets, are easily sexed, very personable birds and, once acclimatized, prove hardy in aviary surroundings.

If you are seeking a pet, but do not feel able to cope with one of the larger and more costly parrots, you will find that some parakeets will develop into very affectionate companions. You can teach them to mimic sounds and voices quite successfully and, provided that you obtain a young bird, there is no reason why you should not have a loyal pet for many years. Although parakeets do not live as long as some of their larger relatives (some parrots outlive their owners), the lifespan of a pet can usually be measured in decades.

Choosing a parakeet

Where you buy your parakeets will depend to some extent on the species you are looking for. Pet stores that specialize in birds are likely to have the largest range available apart from the bird farms, which advertize in the various birdkeeping journals.

Pet shops generally stock a selection of the South American parakeets, simply because these birds will settle well as pets, especially if you obtain them as youngsters. Australian parakeets, on the other hand, usually prove very nervous when caged, and may attempt to fly off when approached or they may retreat to a far corner of the cage.

The true beauty of parakeets is best seen in an aviary with plenty of flying space, and you may wish, therefore, to visit a local breeder before you decide which species to buy. There are many birdkeeping clubs and these can be a useful starting point in contacting a breeder. Joining such a club will also enable you to share experience and knowledge with other members. Often, club members have reciprocal arrangements for looking after each other's birds, for example during holiday periods. Such experienced help can be invaluable, especially if the birds are nesting, or fall ill during your absence. Should you have difficulty in finding your local club, the library may be able to provide the name and address of the secretary. Birdkeeping magazines may also carry advertisements for societies.

Buying imported parakeets

It is important to ask whether the parakeets you are thinking about buying have been imported or whether they were home bred. Although they may be slightly cheaper, imported parakeets, irrespective of their origin, will be more demanding to manage than home-bred stock. Bear in mind that, although such birds will have been quarantined, they are unlikely to be fully acclimatized.

In various parts of the world, wild parakeets cause serious damage to growing crops by feeding on the ripening seeds. Moustached Parakeets, for example, have been known to attack rice crops, just before harvesting, in flocks of thousands. Rather than kill these birds, a number of countries export them under strict welfare and conservation controls. On arrival in the country of import, the birds undergo a period of quarantine before being released for sale to birdkeepers.

Australia presently bans the movement of native birds overseas, even if they have been bred in captivity. However, because Australian parakeets have proved so prolific in aviary surroundings in other countries, large numbers of captive birds are traded internationally every year. Again, they are quarantined in the

Below: *Allow yourself plenty of time to look at the birds in the aviary, and remember to closely examine your chosen bird, before you make a firm decision to buy.*

Above: *The age of the parakeets is important. With Australian species especially, it may be better to start with young birds rather than purchase adult stock.*

importing country, under official control, before being transferred to new aviaries.

If you do buy imported parakeets, you will probably need to keep them in heated accommodation, rather than in an outside aviary, over their first winter. This could present difficulties and will almost certainly mean extra expenditure. The best time to buy imported birds is in the early summer, when the risk of frost will have passed and it will be safe to house them outdoors immediately.

It is unlikely that imported parakeets will breed until the following year, as it will take time for them to adjust to the change in their environment. A few species, notably king parakeets, appear to take much longer than this, however. (When a number of these island races were imported in 1972, it was four years before the birds started nesting. At least six British breeders successfully reared chicks during 1976.)

The significance of age
Once parakeets have moulted into adult plumage, there is no reliable way of ageing them properly unless they are banded and wearing a closed ring, which can only be fitted while the bird is a young chick. After this stage, the parakeet's toes are too large for the ring to be slid over them.

These rings are circular bands of metal, made either of aluminium or stainless steel. The information coded onto a ring may include the year in which the chick hatches (e.g.'89'), the ring number, which identifies the individual bird, and the breeder's initials.

It is obviously helpful to know the age of a parakeet if you wish to breed from it, although some birds are known to have bred successfully well into their twenties. With imported stock, you may decide to choose birds that you can recognize as youngsters. They naturally become much tamer in aviary surroundings than adult birds and this increases the likelihood of successful breeding. Many parakeets are mature at a year old, and even those, such as the psittaculids, which are slower to mature, will normally start breeding by three years of age.

The major problem with buying young parakeets is that they are still likely to be in immature plumage and may, therefore, be difficult to sex.

There are various sexing methods available, in particular chromosomal karyotyping, that are useful for sexing both young birds and adults of species where there is no visual distinction between the sexes.

A problem with buying young parakeets from a single breeder is that it is often difficult to obtain unrelated stock. Never be tempted to purchase birds from the same nest to pair together as this gives very little genetic diversity. Any weaknesses in these parakeets are likely to be magnified in their chicks, and problems such as low fertility and hatchability may become apparent.

Unless you can find a proven pair – and few breeders will part with their best breeding stock unless they are genuinely reducing their collection – you are more likely to encounter problems with newly purchased adult birds than with youngsters. Some cocks, particularly those of Australian species, are very aggressive both to a potential mate and to their chicks and, in some cases, may even kill the hen or chicks. Sadly, there is no effective means of curtailing the instincts of a murderous cock and any new hen will always be at risk. In the case of the psittaculids, it is the hen that is the dominant partner for most of the year. A few cock birds prove too nervous to approach the hens at the beginning of the breeding season when there is a subtle switch in their relationship. The only sure way to avoid these distressing problems is to purchase only proven pairs. If you do buy odd birds, try to obtain a proven cock.

Choosing healthy stock
Start by watching the parakeets on offer for a few minutes. They should appear lively and alert, especially when you approach their cage or aviary. If you are satisfied with their overall appearance, ask the vendor to catch any that

particularly interest you so that you can examine them at close quarters before deciding which, if any, to purchase. It is quite easy to examine parakeets properly, provided that the bird is held correctly so that it cannot struggle.

Do not worry too much about the plumage of imported parakeets as this will be replaced at the next moult. (Parakeets moult annually, usually just after the breeding season.) Many parakeets have long tails, which are easily damaged by careless handling and may be soiled while the birds are in transit. The opportunity to bathe will lead to an instant improvement in feather condition, and a good diet will help to ensure that the new plumage is healthy and sleek.

If you are considering young stock and the birds appear to have difficulty in flying, you will need to check their flight feathers. Ask the vendor to hold the wing open for you so that you can see if there are any primary flight feathers missing. Like budgerigars, parakeets can be afflicted with the viral disease known as French moult, which affects the flight feathers. Grass parakeets are particularly vulnerable, but some studs of Ring-necked Parakeets have also been infected with this disease in recent years. As there is presently no cure for this condition, you should avoid any infected birds. It would also be sensible to refrain from buying any parakeets that have been in contact with French moult, in case they are also infected.

Right: *Check the flight feathers to make sure that none are missing, which could be indicative of French moult. The wing stripe, visible here, can sometimes be of value in sexing Australian species.*

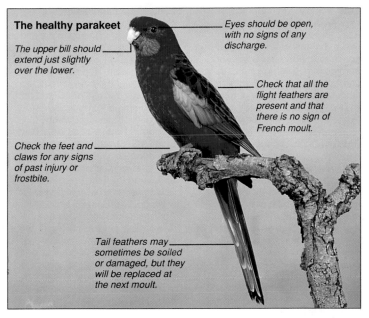

The healthy parakeet

The upper bill should extend just slightly over the lower.

Eyes should be open, with no signs of any discharge.

Check that all the flight feathers are present and that there is no sign of French moult.

Check the feet and claws for any signs of past injury or frostbite.

Tail feathers may sometimes be soiled or damaged, but they will be replaced at the next moult.

The means by which the virus spreads is still unclear, but nest litter may be a source of infection, according to some research reports. Feather loss occurs just after the birds have left the nest. In some cases the feathers may regrow normally, but they often show traces of dried blood in the shaft when inspected closely. The tail feathers may also be lost in severe cases. (Remember, however, that these feathers in young birds are invariably shorter than those of adults, so this alone need not be a cause for concern.)

Occasionally, the flight feathers of parakeets are clipped, as a means of restricting their flight (see page 19). This does not impair their flying ability on a permanent basis, as the cut feathers will be replaced at the next moult.

Look closely at the parakeet's nostrils to check that there is no sign of any discharge. The Australian species appear to suffer more than other parakeets from mycoplasmal infections, which may remain relatively inconspicuous until the bird is stressed, when a more obvious discharge from the nostrils is likely to occur. This

Above: *This Pennant's Parakeet is in excellent feather condition; (feather-plucking can be a problem in this species). Unfortunately, there is no way of aging these birds once they are in adult plumage.*

disease, which may also affect the eyes, can be difficult to eliminate properly, and recurrences are not uncommon. Keep an eye on young birds, which are likely to be infected while still in the nest.

The nostrils should be even in size; a grossly enlarged nostril is a probable sign of a long-standing mycoplasmal infection. The surrounding cere is quite prominent, especially in grass parakeets, and may show some abrasions, particularly in young birds. This need not be a cause for concern, as minor scratches are often caused by the bird flying into the aviary mesh and will heal without problems. Recently fledged grass parakeets often fail to appreciate the confines of their aviary when they first leave the nest, and may fly about wildly at the slightest disturbance.

Check the beak to ensure that it is not deformed in any way.

Occasionally, the upper mandible may grow inside the lower, giving rise to what is known as an undershot beak. This is largely confined to the grass parakeets and, as it may be an inherited characteristic, you should not use such birds for breeding purposes.

Overgrowth of the beak is more likely to arise in pet parakeets if they are deprived of branches on which to gnaw. *Brotogeris* parakeets, particularly, need to be provided with wood on which they can exercise their beaks regularly.

Damage to the beak, such as holes in its surface, may be the result of fighting. Provided that the damage is not too severe, it should heal over a short period of time.

Look particularly closely at the beaks of the New Zealand parakeets, or kakarikis. These birds are particularly prone to a mite infestation, commonly known in budgerigars as 'scaly face' (see pages 40-1). The earliest signs of infestation are small, snail-like tracks over the upper mandible, rapidly developing into swellings that resemble coral growths. In severe cases, these swellings will even spread over much of the body, beneath the plumage.

In some cases, the legs and feet may be infested with mites, too, so check for similar signs here. Look out also for swellings on the toes or in the ball of the foot; any abnormality here could be indicative of injury or infection. The parakeet should have a full complement of claws, especially if you want to exhibit it in the future. Psittaculid species are particularly at risk from frostbite, which can lead to loss of claws and, in severe cases, part of a toe as well. This is serious, because, although the bird may show no sign of discomfort, it may have difficulty in mating.

You can obtain quite a reliable indication of the parakeet's overall condition by examining the breastbone. This runs in the midline of the lower chest as a bony prominence. You will be able to locate it quite easily by moving your finger down over this part of the body. If the parakeet is in good condition, you should be able to feel the bone as a slight bony ridge, with well-developed muscle on either side. In an ailing bird, the muscles waste and hollows form on each side of the bone. A bird in such a condition is described as 'going light', and, especially in young Australian parakeets, this can be indicative of a heavy burden of intestinal worms or, sometimes, of a more serious condition.

It is always advisable to ask if and when the parakeets were dewormed, and which drug was used. Most breeders, especially of Australian species, have a regular deworming programme (see pages 41-2), but the most effective means of control is to try to prevent such parasites from gaining access to your aviaries. You can do this by screening the droppings of new birds before releasing them into the main aviary. Your veterinarian will undertake this investigation for you and will also prescribe the necessary treatment. Alternatively, you may decide to deworm all birds, as a matter of course, during their quarantine period with you. By keeping them apart from your established stock, you can make sure that they have settled in properly and are healthy. A quarantine period of about 14 days should be adequate.

Below: *This young Adelaide Rosella is suffering from French moult; note the stunted feathering.*

Transporting parakeets

It is always best to move parakeets in a box, rather than use a cage, as they will settle better in the dark. Cardboard boxes are satisfactory for small species, such as grass parakeets, but are quite unsuitable for *Brotogeris* and psittaculid species, which will chew their way out of the box on the journey home, using the ventilation holes as a starting point. If you are forced to use a cardboard box in an emergency, be certain to place the ventilation holes at the top of the box, which, hopefully, will be out of reach of the birds. You should also check that both the top and bottom of the box are securely closed and taped, since the parakeets could escape through an opening here.

A purpose-built wooden box, with ventilation holes, is ideal for transporting parakeets home, and will also be useful for moving birds from the aviary to an inside flight. If you fit a carrying handle on the top of the box, make certain that it is secure enough to hold the weight.

If you are travelling with parakeets in a car, avoid putting them on the back seat, where they could be exposed to direct sunlight. Fumes from the engine and excessive heat can be fatal within minutes. If you have to stop on the way home, remember that the temperature within the vehicle can increase very rapidly, so do not leave the birds alone.

Choosing parakeets for the home and garden

Group	Suitability as pets	Suitability as aviary birds
Grass parakeets	Too nervous.	Check for French moult. Deworming is necessary.
Larger Australian parakeets	As above, although some hand-reared rosellas can become reasonably tame.	Cocks can prove very aggressive. Look closely for runny noses and swollen eyes. Again, deworming is vital.
Psittaculid parakeets	Are often shy of close contact since they're not a pair-bonding species.	Watch for signs of French moult. Start with proven pairs if possible. Check the birds' feet; psittaculids are prone to frostbite.
Brotogeris parakeets	Young birds can become very tame and devoted to their owners but can develop jealous natures.	Brotogeris parakeets are best kept in a colony, but introduce all the birds at the same time, otherwise fighting is inevitable.
Bolborhynchus parakeets	Rather shy. Prone to obesity.	Can be difficult to establish, so obtain acclimatized or captive-bred stock if possible.
Kakarikis	These active birds will not settle in cage surroundings.	Watch for scaly-face.

Housing parakeets in the home

Cages are not really suitable for many parakeets; most of the Australian species, in particular, are too nervous and their tails are too easily damaged, for them to be kept satisfactorily in confined surroundings, but there are cage designs that are suitable for the *Brotogeris* species. Choose a large model, as they are active birds, but check that the gap between the bars is not too great, otherwise the birds could become caught up. They will also be more at risk from cats, if you have any, especially when you are out of the room.

A metal cage is most suitable, since many parakeets are surprisingly destructive and will rapidly destroy a wooden cage. A budgerigar flight cage is suitable for them, especially if you choose one of the modular systems, which you can enlarge by connecting additional units of the same basic design to the original one.

Some cages may have plastic bases, but these are usually positioned so that the parakeets do not gnaw at them, and you can distract their attention from the base by providing wooden branches as perches, which they can gnaw, and which you can replace easily.

Alternatively, you may wish to obtain a small indoor aviary. An increasing number of stylish designs are being produced, some of which are mounted on castors, which facilitates cleaning. Because these units are invariably taller than

A double-tiered flight cage for parakeets

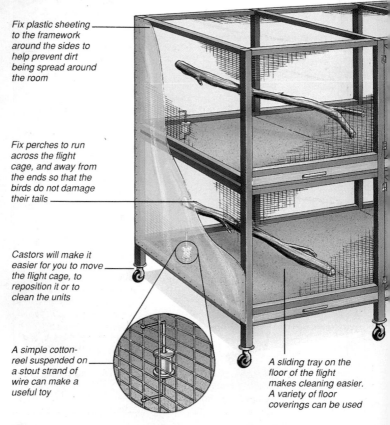

Fix plastic sheeting to the framework around the sides to help prevent dirt being spread around the room

Fix perches to run across the flight cage, and away from the ends so that the birds do not damage their tails

Castors will make it easier for you to move the flight cage, to reposition it or to clean the units

A simple cotton-reel suspended on a stout strand of wire can make a useful toy

A sliding tray on the floor of the flight makes cleaning easier. A variety of floor coverings can be used

traditional cages, they are quite suitable for long-tailed parakeets, such as the Alexandrine or Ring-necked species.

An indoor aviary of this type is also useful for accommodating recently imported birds over the winter period, or for housing young birds when they first become independent.

Siting the cage
To help birds feel secure in their new environment, position the cage alongside a wall, possibly in the corner of a room. Once a parakeet is tame, it may not mind being moved to a more central location. Avoid draughty spots, such as hallways, and never place the cage where it is exposed to direct sunlight, in front of a window, for example, as overheating could be fatal to the birds.

It is a good idea to screen the back of the cage with a polythene shield to protect the wall-covering from becoming stained with droppings or pieces of fruit, which the birds will scatter outside the cage. Allow a small gap between the cage and the screen so that the birds cannot damage it.

Ideally, you should position the parakeets' quarters so that the birds perch just below eye level. This will help them to become used to you, and will thus facilitate the taming process. It will also prevent you having to stoop to open the cage door, and the birds will feel more secure in a higher position with a better view of the room.

Although you can buy special stands for smaller cage designs, many tend to be rather unstable and are easily toppled over. They are clearly not recommended if you have young children in the house. A piece of furniture will often make a better base. If the cage is equipped with castors, you will need to ensure that the floor is level, or lock the castors in place with a wedge, to prevent the cage from sliding forward into the room.

Preparing the cage
Always wash a new cage thoroughly before placing the parakeets inside. Never use metal polish of any kind on the bars or elsewhere in the cage as this may be harmful to the birds. Parakeets often spend long periods of time, even in a spacious aviary, climbing around on the wire, and can easily ingest the remains of polish or other substances. If you want to clean the bars thoroughly, use one of the special wipes marketed for this purpose, which are available from pet stores. Alternatively, scrub the cage with a disinfectant solution that is safe for use with pets, and then rinse it thoroughly. It is best to do this outdoors, using a hose-pipe to ensure that it is really clean.

Dry the various parts of the cage with paper towelling, taking care

Young parakeets enjoy running up a ladder, but be sure they can not become stuck between the rungs

Include a separate door panel for ease of access to the interior

that no droplets of water remain, especially on the plastic. (If the cage is allowed to dry naturally, stubborn water marks will remain on the surface, which may be hard to remove.) You can then reassemble the cage in readiness for the parakeets. Preparing their quarters can take some time, so, if possible, buy the birds only when everything is ready for them.

Floor coverings
It is usual to cover the floor of the cage, so that it will be easy to clean. For indoor use, sandsheets are a popular choice as they look reasonably attractive and are quite absorbent. Unfortunately, they tend to be manufactured to fit specific sizes of cage and are not available to cover the larger bases of most flight units. You can place a number of sheets over the floor area, folding or cutting them to fit, but the birds will probably scatter them on top of each other, leaving areas of the floor uncovered. You may have to hold the pieces of sandsheet together with adhesive tape fixed on the lower paper surface of the sandsheet, where it will stick more effectively and be concealed out of the parakeets' reach. Some birds resort to shredding their sandsheets, most notably when they are in breeding condition. This is normally not a problem, but if the behaviour persists, you may have to find a temporary alternative.

Bird sand is obtainable from most pet shops and is often mixed with grit. It is relatively heavy to carry, but cheaper than sandsheets. You will need to sprinkle a thick layer over the floor of the cage so that there is an adequate covering, otherwise droppings will stick to the floor of the cage making it difficult to clean. The parakeets may peck around on the floor, but this will cause no problems and they should benefit from the grit mixed in with the sand.

Newspaper, the cheapest floor covering, acts as an efficient cover and can be disposed of easily, but it does look rather unattractive and,

Above: *A parrot cage housing a pair of Cobalt-winged Parakeets. The detachable plastic base is held in place with metal clips.*

again, the parakeets may be tempted to chew it up. Use only clean sheets and avoid coloured newspapers, in case any of the inks used are toxic to the birds.

Perches
Suitable perches in the cage are vital for the parakeets' well-being. Unfortunately, many cages are fitted with plastic perches, which are totally inadequate and uncomfortable for most birds. Within a few weeks of being placed in a cage with plastic perches, birds will usually spend most of their time clinging onto the side of the enclosure. You should therefore replace plastic or dowelling perches with branches on which the parakeets can gnaw and also exercise their feet.

Because both plastic and dowelling perches fitted in cages are of standard dimensions, allowing the birds no variation in grip, pressure sores are likely to appear on the ball of the foot over a period of time. The condition sometimes described as 'bumblefoot', where these sores become infected, is difficult to cure successfully. Perches for parakeets should be sufficiently thick to enable the birds to grip effectively, without the claws from the front and hind toes touching each other.

Branches from a variety of trees make suitable perches; fruit trees, such as apple, sycamore and elder, are all suitable. Parakeets will often swallow some of the bark, which they strip off the branches, so avoid lilac, yew and laburnum, which will be poisonous, and check on other trees before you use branches from them. It is also important to ensure that any branches you use have not been sprayed with potentially harmful chemicals.

Use fresh-cut branches rather than dead wood because there is less risk of them developing a fungus. Strip off any leaves, but leave the sideshoots, as the parakeets will enjoy nipping off these. It is a good idea to wash the branches before placing them in the cage, in case they have been contaminated, for example by the droppings of wild birds.

Fix the perches across, rather than along, the cage to allow the birds the maximum flying space.

Above: *Some parakeets, such as this Cobaltwing, enjoy climbing the cage bars. Make sure you also provide fresh-cut branch perches.*

You should also ensure that the perches are positioned so that the birds' tails avoid contact with the mesh. Otherwise, the tail feathers are likely to become frayed, which will result in the parakeets' whole appearance being spoilt.

Cut the branches slightly longer than the width of the cage and fix them at an angle. Having stripped off the bark, the parakeets are likely to gnaw at the ends of their perches and, if you have cut them to fit, they will soon be too short. If you allow extra length when you cut them, you can adjust their position later as necessary.

Should you decide to use strands of wire to support the perches in the cage, make sure that they are coiled very tightly around each end of the branch to prevent the birds' claws catching in the wire. Ideally, attach the perches so that you can easily remove them. You will then be able to wash them outside the cage, causing the minimum of disturbance to the parakeets.

Toys

Some cages are equipped with a swing, but birds seldom show much enthusiasm for what is in effect an unstable perch! You could leave a swing in place, but most parakeets will prefer to use a high perch for roosting at night.

The many toys produced for budgerigars are rarely suitable for parakeets. With their more destructive natures, they will destroy them quite rapidly, and may expose sharp projections on plastic toys, on which they can easily injure themselves.

You may wish to buy some of the wooden toys that are now being marketed for parrots. These are usually quite safe, but remember that they are likely to be destroyed in time and will need replacing.

Alternatively, you can make your own toys quite easily. A wooden cotton reel, with the labels removed, is ideal. Another popular toy is easy to make by drilling a hole through the centre of a number of small squares of softwood timber and threading these onto a stout strand of wire. Place the 'toy' inside the cage and secure the ends of the wire on the outside of the bars. The parakeet will enjoy sliding the wood up and down on the wire and chewing it, and you can easily slide off soiled and broken blocks to replace them as necessary.

Young *Brotogeris* parakeets appreciate a ladder in their quarters, and one of the stout ladders designed for budgerigars may be suitable. If you decide to make one, using lengths of dowelling, check that the spacing between the rungs is not too wide, or there is a risk that a parakeet may become stuck trying to climb between rungs.

Because of their sociable natures, members of this group often favour a mirror. Unfortunately, the plastic designs used for budgerigars are not sufficiently robust to withstand the beaks of *Brotogeris* parakeets for long, but you may be able to lengthen the life of this toy by hanging it on the outside of the cage, near a perch.

Similarly, plastic open-weave toy balls, often used in budgerigar cages, will soon be destroyed. They are also very easily soiled by droppings and difficult to clean. Instead, give the birds a table-tennis ball; they will have difficulty in puncturing it as there are no exposed edges and it will also be much easier to clean.

Many parakeets seem to enjoy the companionship of a radio, which will help to occupy them while you are out. They rarely show a definite preference for either music or discussion programmes!

Taming your parakeet

A parakeet that you have obtained as a youngster should be quite tame, especially if it has been raised by hand, and it will probably be easy to train to feed from your hand. Pieces of fruit and peanuts in their shells are very useful during the taming process, since most birds like such food. Holding the food in your fingers, offer it directly to the bird. If the parakeet is reluctant to eat from your hand,

Above: *Hold the parakeet's head between your index and middle fingers, taking care not to press on the bird's neck.*

place the fruit in the food pot, where the bird will almost certainly retrieve it, and repeat the process on the following day. Gradually, the bird will overcome its shyness, initially grabbing the food from your hand, then, as it grows in confidence, taking the food more readily. The length of time it will take you to reach this stage will vary according to the age and origins of the bird. Nevertheless, the longer you can spend with your pet, the sooner you can anticipate results from your efforts .

Although most parakeets are not very talented talkers, you should still be able to teach them a few words and phrases if you repeat the words regularly. Start with a simple name, such as 'Joey', and then add 'Hello' every time you enter the room. Once your pet has learnt these words, add another basic phrase, and expand the bird's vocabulary accordingly.

Young birds will readily accept your outstretched finger as an extension of their perch. Gently encourage them to do this by placing your index finger parallel with the perch. Then slowly move your finger to touch the parakeet's toes, until the bird steps onto your hand. Soon it will come to perch there readily without any fear and, depending on the height of the cage door, you should be able to move the bird out while it is still on perched on your finger.

Parakeets like to explore a room, but it is advisable to wait until your pet is finger-tame before you let it out for the first time so that you will be able to return it to its cage without difficulty. Before you let the parakeet out into the room, ensure that windows are closed, and screened with net curtains, so that the parakeet will not attempt to fly through the glass. You should also put away ornaments, any plants that could prove poisonous if eaten and shut out dogs and cats.

Never leave a parakeet alone in the room while it is out of its cage. Apart from the damage it could inflict on itself, its beak could make a lasting impression on furniture, or inflict a devastating bite on a live electrical flex.

You may wish to place special perches in the room, which the parakeet will soon learn to recognize when flying around. Place paper beneath the perches to catch any droppings. A parakeet will also enjoy perching on your shoulder, but be careful that it does not nip your ear lobe, as this can be a very painful experience!

Below: Brotogeris *species can develop into very tame pets if you obtain them at an early age, and will even feed from your hand.*

Wing-clipping

Wing-clipping may be necessary for the safety or health of a parakeet or that of its mate. Restricting its flight in this way will prevent the parakeet injuring itself by flying directly into, or escaping via, a window if one is left open by accident. Wing-clipping handicaps a parakeet until the cut feathers are moulted out. Provided that only one wing is clipped, the parakeet will retain some flying ability, and the process itself is quite painless.

You will need a sharp pair of blunt-ended scissors for clipping the wings and, preferably, someone else to hold the parakeet. Open the wing out and locate the primary flight feathers, which run along the rear edge. Leaving the outer two intact, start cutting the remainder in a straight line at a point just above the shaft. The feathering here is dead, as it has no blood supply; if you cut the feather nearer to the body, where it is growing, there is a strong likelihood of serious bleeding. Should you be in any doubt, ask your veterinarian for advice.

Birdkeepers sometimes clip the wings of a cock that is proving aggressive towards its mate. This ensures that the hen can fly with greater speed than the cock, and is unlikely to be pinned down in one part of the aviary by him.

Housing parakeets in the garden

At its most basic, an aviary is comprised of an enclosed shelter and an attached flight area, which is constructed of wire mesh on a wooden framework. If you do not have the time or the skill to build an aviary yourself, a large number of firms now specialize in producing aviaries in kit form, which are easy to assemble on a ready prepared base. The advantage of purchasing a sectional structure is that if you need to move house during this period, you can dismantle the aviary quite easily, and re-erect it elsewhere with the minimum of problems. Some firms will even erect the aviary for you.

You may even find it cheaper to purchase an aviary in sectional form than to build your own, particularly if you are interested in the grass parakeets, or other less destructive species, such as members of the *Bolborhynchus* genus. Ask at your local pet store for the names of aviary suppliers near where you live, or trace them through their advertisements in the various birdkeeping magazines.

Always try to visit a manufacturers' premises before making any choice, so that you can see the standard of workmanship for yourself. A straightforward comparison of prices can be misleading if you don't examine closely what is on offer. Look, for example, at the thickness of timber used, and the gauge and spacing of the mesh. Jointed panels should prove more durable than those made of lengths of timber that are simply nailed together. Mesh should be fixed securely to the framework using special netting staples, rather than simply tacked in place with battening.

Some manufacturers offer untreated frames. Although coating with a safe weather-proofing agent will increase the price, it will also extend the lifespan of the structure.

Right: *Most parakeets need to be kept in individual pairs when breeding, but you may be able to house them together in groups for the rest of the year.*

A good aviary, that is properly maintained from the outset, should last for well over a decade.

Siting the aviary
Where you site the aviary in your garden is an important consideration. The parakeets will benefit from being kept in a sheltered and relatively secluded place, so try to avoid positioning the aviary where it will be exposed to the prevailing winds. During the winter months, the effects of the so-called 'wind-chill' factor will expose the birds to much lower temperatures than if they were in a more sheltered spot. A site within view of the house would be agreeable and is especially advantageous if you want to have access to amenities such as water and electricity. A level site will make construction much easier.

Although they act as a windbreak, trees can be dangerous, especially if branches fall on the aviary. A more commonly encountered disadvantage, however, is that they provide cats with an easy means of reaching the aviary. This can be catastrophic, especially during the breeding period, as, although the cats may not be able to harm the parakeets directly, they can cause the birds to desert their nest, which often results in the death of the young chicks, especially after dark. You may, therefore, need to trim back trees in order to accommodate an aviary.

Above: *Blocks of flights, such as these attractive ones, need to be double wired to prevent parakeets inflicting injuries to the feet of birds in adjoining aviaries.*

To avoid disturbing your garden more than necessary, try to plan the aviary to fit on a site near an existing path. (You will need to walk to the aviary every day and will want to avoid muddy patches on the lawn.) If you have children, it is a good idea to avoid their main play area, since noise close to the aviary is bound to disturb even the most committed breeding pairs.

A site next to a garden pond is also inappropriate. Apart from the possibility of flooding during periods of heavy rainfall, the birds may suffer from biting midges, which breed in the pond water.

Finally, it is always advisable to check with your local planning department before starting to build an aviary, even though, under most circumstances, official permission is not required. You should also inform your neighbours.

Constructing an aviary

The size of the aviary will depend to a great extent on the species, and the number of pairs, that you intend to keep. For a pair of grass parakeets, a standard-sized flight is 270cm(9ft) long, 90cm(3ft) wide and 180cm(6ft) high, connected to a 90cm(3ft) square shelter of similar height. The psittaculid parakeets, broadtails or rosellas, and other larger Australasian species, will show to better effect in a flight at least 360cm(12ft) in length, and longer if space permits.

When the parakeets are kept in small groups the width of the aviary should be increased to give the birds adequate flying space. An aviary 180cm(6ft) wide is ideal. It is a good idea to plan the size of your first aviary so that you can expand easily on the same site at a later date, if you wish. It is not unusual for parakeet aviaries to be arranged in blocks and serviced from a corridor at the back of the structure (see page 27). This is a far more economical proposition, both in terms of space and finance, than building several aviaries scattered around the garden.

It is best to build your aviary when the weather is fine, as frost prevents mortar from drying properly. The late summer is probably the most suitable time of year to build. Hopefully, you will then have completed the structure by early autumn and, if you are purchasing home-bred stock, you can transfer the parakeets directly to their new quarters to settle in over the winter. They may then be ready to start nesting by the springtime, whereas if they are placed in strange surroundings in the spring, it is likely to be a further year before they show serious signs of breeding.

First, you will need to clear the site, and roughly level it as necessary. You can cut out some of the turf with a sharp spade, and store it in the shade to replant around the perimeter of the aviary once you have completed the work.

You will need to mark out the dimensions of the structure carefully before you excavate the footings that form the exterior boundaries; use a trail of sand or string on stakes. Secure foundations are vital, irrespective of the size of the aviary; they not only help to anchor the structure firmly in position, but also prevent the woodwork rotting prematurely. Blockwork, set to a depth of approximately 30cm(12in) below ground level, and rising to a similar height above, will form the base on which the aviary will rest. It is also usual to put a dividing layer of blocks across the aviary to support the entrance to the shelter.

Prepare the floor of the aviary before setting the frames in place. Although the idea of a grass floor may be an attractive one, it is rarely

Preparing the site

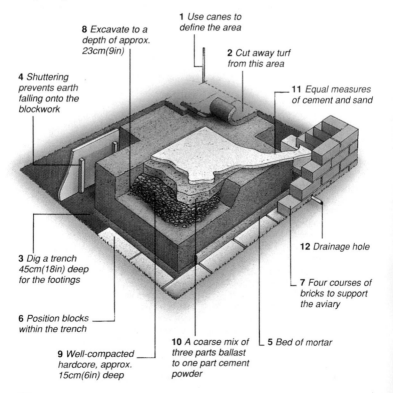

1 *Use canes to define the area*

2 *Cut away turf from this area*

8 *Excavate to a depth of approx. 23cm(9in)*

4 *Shuttering prevents earth falling onto the blockwork*

11 *Equal measures of cement and sand*

3 *Dig a trench 45cm(18in) deep for the footings*

12 *Drainage hole*

7 *Four courses of bricks to support the aviary*

6 *Position blocks within the trench*

9 *Well-compacted hardcore, approx. 15cm(6in) deep*

10 *A coarse mix of three parts ballast to one part cement powder*

5 *Bed of mortar*

practical unless the aviary is very large. Parasitic worm infestations (see page 41) will be much easier to eliminate from a solid base, which is easy to wash down. A concrete base will also help to hold the blockwork firmly in position and should ensure that rats and foxes cannot tunnel into the aviary and harm the birds.

Paving slabs are an alternative to concrete, and look more attractive, but you must ensure that you position the slabs correctly, so that water will drain off rather than settling in puddles. With concrete, it is easier to set up an adequate gradient, which will allow the rainwater to drain away from the shelter and out of the aviary through a drainage hole set at the end of the flight.

Some parakeet breeders favour a gravel base to the flight. A dense layer, at least 15cm/6in deep, of gravel chips covers a bed of clinker, which assists drainage. The gravel acts rather like a filter bed, with rainwater washing the droppings down between the chips. It is a good idea to set a paving slab in the gravel beneath any perches located under cover to make cleaning easier.

Unfortunately, if the parakeets are infested with intestinal worms, it will be as difficult to eliminate the worm eggs from the gravel as from grass. The flight will also be difficult to clean thoroughly during the moulting period, when feathers accumulate on the floor. Spilt food, such as greenstuff or fruit brought from the shelter, will attract the birds to the floor, where they will be at risk from infections such as pseudotuberculosis, which thrives under the damp conditions of a gravel base. The base of the aviary is a particularly important consideration if you intend to keep Australian parakeets as, unlike most other parakeets, which usually prefer to feed at perch levels, they regularly descend to the ground in search of food. These species will therefore be particularly vulnerable to such bacterial infections.

The flight

It is an easy matter to order flight panels that are ready for assembly, and these will enable you to press on rapidly with building the aviary. If you do decide to build your own panels, however, then order the timber cut to size. Aviary flights tend to be built around dimensions of 90cm(3ft), simply because mesh is most commonly available in sheets of this size.

It is possible to buy timber that has been treated with a weather-proofing agent, but do make sure that this is safe for use with livestock. If in doubt, buy untreated timber, and paint the lengths with a couple of coats of a safe product, allowing it to dry thoroughly before making it up into frames. You can treat the cut ends of timber as you assemble the frames.

Nineteen-gauge mesh will be adequate for the smaller Australian species, including the Red-rumped Parakeet, but thicker, 16-gauge mesh is recommended for other parakeets. This is more durable, and the birds will not be able to destroy it by gnawing at it with their beaks. If you are buying ready-made panels, ensure that the mesh is of the appropriate thickness, even if it adds slightly to the cost.

The actual dimensions of the strands of mesh are also significant, to prevent small rodents, especially mice, gaining access to the aviary. Mesh measuring 2.5x1.25cm(1x0.5in) should exclude them, but 1.25cm(0.5in)-square mesh will give greater security. This, of course, is more costly, but, bearing in mind the damage and disturbance that mice can cause in an aviary, it is a worthwhile investment, especially in areas where mice are prevalent.

By planning the panels to fit the mesh, you will avoid wastage and the need to trim the sides. You can contact discount suppliers of aviary mesh through their advertisements, which frequently appear in birdkeeping magazines, but you should be able to obtain suitable mesh from large DIY stores.

Above: *1.25cm(0.5in) square mesh. Thin 19(G) gauge.*

Above: *1.25cm(0.5in) square mesh. Thicker 16(G) gauge.*

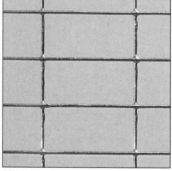

Above: *2.5x1.25cm(1x0.5in) mesh. Thin 19(G) gauge.*

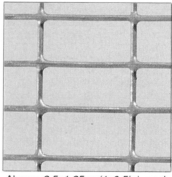

Above: *2.5x1.25cm(1x0.5in) mesh. Thicker 16(G) gauge.*

Start by laying the frames flat on a level surface, then carefully unroll the mesh and tack it roughly in place down the frame. You can make any necessary adjustments later, before you secure the mesh to the frames with bolts. Keep the mesh taut, so that it does not sag, and ensure that the sides of the mesh run parallel with the framework, otherwise the final appearance of the aviary will be spoilt. It is useful to allow a slight overlap of mesh at the top and bottom of the frame, especially for the more destructive parakeets. You can then hammer the extra lengths onto the adjoining faces, and tack them in place here, too. When the panels are assembled, all the timber will be protected and there will be no need for battening.

For an aviary to house grass parakeets, you can simply cut the mesh, having fixed the lengths in place on the frame, and use thin, 2.5x1.25cm(1x0.5in) battening to cover, and thus protect the birds from, the sharp ends of mesh.

A particular problem that you may encounter with *Brotogeris* parakeets, housed in flights made of 2.5x1.25(1x0.5in) mesh, is that they can use their beaks to reach the timber of the framework directly through the mesh. It may be worthwhile wrapping the upper part of the frame with thinner, 19-gauge mesh, and then applying the aviary mesh on top in the normal manner. You will probably need longer netting staples for this purpose. Although this may seem a rather tiresome precaution, it is much harder to solve the problem once the parakeets have destroyed the framework from within. (They are even capable of removing netting staples by gnawing around them.)

Fix the panels together with bolts, remembering to use washers and to oil the nuts so that they will be easy to remove later, should you need to move the aviary. The wired surface should always form the inner surface of the flight once the panels are assembled. Place the frames on a bed of mortar and fasten them to the blocks by means of frame-fixers. Finally, you can bolt the roofing panels in place. They should fit easily on top of the structure, with the bolts dropping down through the horizontal bars of the panels beneath.

The shelter

There has been a trend during recent years to use a raised shelter as an attachment to the parakeet flight. The major advantage is financial; it is much cheaper to build a raised box, supported on legs, than a full-length structure.

The raised shelter should be about 90cm(3ft) from the ground

Plans for aviaries with shelters and safety porches

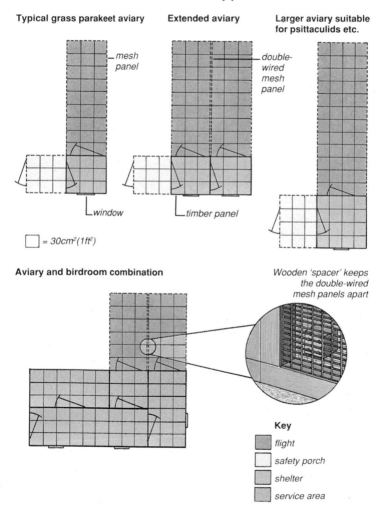

Typical grass parakeet aviary — mesh panel, window

Extended aviary — timber panel

Larger aviary suitable for psittaculids etc. — double-wired mesh panel

☐ = 30cm²(1ft²)

Aviary and birdroom combination

Wooden 'spacer' keeps the double-wired mesh panels apart

Key
- flight
- safety porch
- shelter
- service area

and should be the same width as the aviary. In most cases, therefore, it will be in the form of a 90cm(3ft) cube. Make this shelter in sectional form, using either thick-exterior plywood or tongued-and-grooved timber. Cover the interior of the sides and the roof with wire mesh to prevent the parakeets from gaining access to the timber and gnawing their way out of the aviary.

Although you can support the shelter on wooden legs, it will be quite a heavy structure and so brick pillars are more suitable for the purpose. Build the supports first, so that they will be dry by the time that the shelter is finished, and set a supporting frame on top before fixing the shelter itself in place.

Where the shelter connects to the flight you will need to attach a horizontal wooden bar, about 90cm(3ft) from ground level, to the corresponding frame of the flight and cover the gap beneath the shelter with mesh. You can also bolt the wooden frame of the shelter to the framework of the flight to make it even more stable.

The roof of the shelter can be in the form of an apex, but is more

A typical parakeet aviary with raised shelter

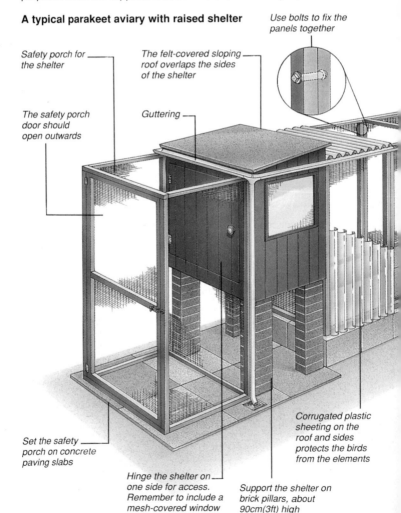

Use bolts to fix the panels together

Safety porch for the shelter

The felt-covered sloping roof overlaps the sides of the shelter

The safety porch door should open outwards

Guttering

Set the safety porch on concrete paving slabs

Hinge the shelter on one side for access. Remember to include a mesh-covered window

Support the shelter on brick pillars, about 90cm(3ft) high

Corrugated plastic sheeting on the roof and sides protects the birds from the elements

commonly constructed as a flat, sloping cover, which channels rainwater away from the flight. The roof should overlap all the sides once it is in place, and the roofing felt should also overlap for a short distance. This will help to exclude draughts, as well as keep the rain out. Fix guttering at the back of the shelter to channel the run-off of water away from the safety porch.

Construct the back of the shelter as a separate unit, hinged on one side so that it opens easily to give you full access to the interior.

The parakeets will need an

entrance hole, with a landing platform, to give them access to the shelter from the flight. The size of the entrance will depend to some extent on the size of the parakeets, but usually varies between about 15cm(6in) square for smaller species to 22.5cm(9in) square for the largest psittaculid parakeets. For the platform, cut a piece of plywood to fit the entrance.

There may be a time when you need to close the parakeets either in the shelter or in the flight, for example to help you catch them. Cut a thin piece of plywood fractionally larger than the entrance and drill corresponding holes in the door posts and the cover. You can then hold the plywood over the entrance and screw it in place whenever you need to close off the shelter or flight.

Other housing options

You can, of course, use a garden shed as a shelter, adapting the window space as the entry point to the flight. If you choose one measuring about 240x180cm (8x6ft), you may be able to dispense with a safety porch altogether by fitting an internal wire mesh panel, complete with door, to partition the shed. You can then use the extra under-cover space that this will give you to store seed and equipment.

Developing this idea further, some birdkeepers connect two flights to a single shed, which is also equipped with an indoor flight. This structure, described as a birdroom, offers much greater flexibility than an aviary on its own, especially if it has its own power supply and running water.

Another option is a block of aviaries – each with flight and shelter – that are connected by a service corridor. Here again, a safety porch is unnecessary, as you can enter by the door at the end of the corridor and, provided you only open the doors to the shelters once you have closed the external one, the birds will be safe.

If you will be keeping parakeets in adjoining aviaries, you must

Use netting staples to fix mesh to the frames, and protect cut ends of mesh with battening

Safety porch into the flight

Use 'framefixers' to secure the frames on the footings

Support the flight on concrete footings. Ideally, the floor, too, should be concrete

ensure that the flights are double-wired to prevent the parakeets from reaching each other through the mesh, and injuring their toes fighting. Double-wiring simply means that both sides of the adjoining framework, each of which is covered with mesh, are separated by the width of the timber used to make the frame. It is important that the mesh is fixed tautly to the frames; if it sags, the birds may still be able to reach each other's feet. Beak injuries can also occur if the double-wiring is inadequate and, if a bird's tongue is nipped, bleeding may be serious.

The safety porch
It is important to plan your entry points to the aviary carefully. Parakeets are generally very fast on the wing and may slip past you quite easily unless you have a safety porch to provide a double-door entry system to prevent the birds from escaping. Ideally, there should be a safety porch around the shelter (particularly if you have a raised shelter) as well as around any entry point into the flight. Otherwise, you will be forced to enter the flight each time you feed the parakeets, which will be disturbing for them, particularly during the warmer part of the year when they may be nesting. These mesh porches should measure about 90cm(3ft) square and attach around the door to the aviary. To give you more space, hinge the door of the safety porch to open outwards and the one into the shelter to open inwards.

The birdroom

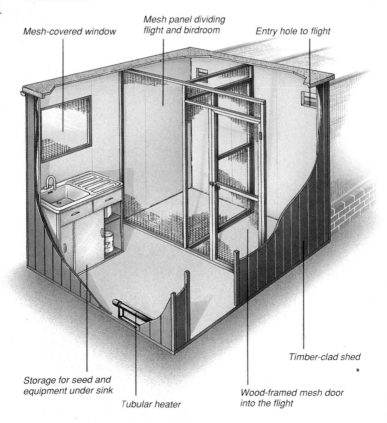

Mesh-covered window

Mesh panel dividing flight and birdroom

Entry hole to flight

Timber-clad shed

Storage for seed and equipment under sink

Tubular heater

Wood-framed mesh door into the flight

Outside cover

Once the aviary is complete, add translucent, corrugated plastic sheeting to the roof and sides of the flight adjoining the shelter. This will provide cover for the parakeets when they are outside during periods of bad weather. Support the plastic on the roof so that rainwater runs off into the flight, rather than dripping into the vicinity of the shelter. Leave part of the flight uncovered, so that the parakeets can bathe when it rains. If you are in a particularly exposed area, you can add tongued-and-grooved timber along one side of the flight as a further protection against the elements. This is especially recommended if you are keeping grass parakeets, which will not thrive in damp, windy surroundings.

Perches

Perches within the shelter should run across the width of the aviary rather than lengthways, and must be fixed firmly in position. You can use branches from a variety of trees (see page 17). Fix the perches in the flight in a similar position, but slightly lower than those in the shelter, to encourage the parakeets to roost indoors. Take care not to clutter the flying space unnecessarily; for most parakeets, perches at each end of the flight will be adequate. You can also include tree-like branches set in pots on the floor of the flight. Hopefully, as they are easier to replace, the birds will use these to sharpen their beaks, and their attention will be diverted from those positioned higher in the aviary.

Heating, lighting and ventilation

Lighting and ventilation are very important, especially in a small shelter. If the interior is too dark, the parakeets will ignore the shelter and roost outside at night, where, in the winter, they will be exposed to the cold and, consequently, susceptible to frost bite.

It is a good idea to include a small inspection window at the back of the shelter and a larger one on one side. If possible, these should be easy to remove. Both windows should, of course, be covered on the inside with mesh. This will mean that, on warm days, you can increase the ventilation by taking the windows out, while the mesh will prevent the parakeets from escaping. The mesh will also prevent the birds attempting to fly through the glass. Grass parakeets are especially at risk and can be fatally injured.

You can overwinter recently imported parakeets quite safely in the indoor flight if you use safe tubular convector heaters. These heaters will also be useful if you are housing young birds that have been separated from their parents. If necessary, you can provide additional light on a time-switch as well. This will enable you to see to the parakeets when it is dark outside. Be careful, however, not to frighten them by turning on a strong light when it is completely dark, or they could injure themselves.

Security precautions

As the cost of the birds has risen significantly during recent years, so the number of thefts has also increased dramatically. If you have a fairly large collection, you may want to investigate the possibilities of insurance. In any case, it is worth attaching a hasp and padlock to all external doors to act as a deterrent to both casual vandals and more dedicated thieves.

It is possible to have birds marked permanently under the wings with a tattoo, but this marking does become blurred over a period of time. A more effective and recent development in the field of identification is the use of microchip implants, which are placed in the bird, usually in the breast muscle, by a veterinarian. The tiny capsule contains all the necessary information required to identify an individual bird, and is read by a special external scanner, passed over the area of the implant. It appears to cause the bird no discomfort, provides a very reliable means of identification, and, of course, its presence is not readily apparent to a thief.

You could also invest in any of a number of security devices around the aviary in the hope of preventing a break-in. For impartial advice on the system best suited to your needs and budget, ask a crime prevention officer from your local police force.

Deterring rodents

Mice and rats remain a constant threat to the birdkeeper but, by careful management, you should be able to discourage these pests. If you store seed in bins, and feed the parakeets in the shelter, rather than in the flight, rodents are less likely to be attracted to the aviary. Good hygiene is also vital, so clean up spilt seed regularly and change the floor covering about twice a week. (If you line the floor of the shelter with sheets of old newspaper, the task becomes very straightforward.)

Even after taking these precautions, you should remain on the watch for rodents in the aviary; they are usually betrayed by their droppings and foul-smelling urine. If you do find evidence of their presence, you will need to take rapid action to eliminate them before they start breeding. With a guaranteed food supply, their rate of reproduction can be quite staggering. A single female mouse may have over 100 offspring in a year and within this period, of course, many of the offspring will be breeding themselves. Apart from eating the bird seed, they represent a health hazard and are likely to interfere with breeding by disturbing the parakeets.

In the first instance, try to find where the mice are gaining access to the aviary. It may be possible to put down poison at this point, out of reach of the parakeets, other animals, and children. Failing this, you can lay traps, some of which are quite safe to use within the aviary itself and can catch a large number of mice at one setting. Suitable traps are often advertised in the birdkeeping magazines. With

the lid left off the trap for several days, the mice are encouraged to enter and feed. When the lid is replaced, the mice can still go in, but find themselves unable to escape from the trap.

Rats are an even greater potential menace than mice; they will maim and even kill birds, seizing them off the perches or frightening them to the floor after dark. They tend to make fairly conspicuous burrows leading into the aviary, and their droppings will be clearly visible if you have a concrete floor. Although you can lay traps for them, it would be much better to seek advice from a pest control specialist.

A good cat should prevent rodents from gaining access to an aviary and, if you catch the parakeets and confine them in the shelter, it will be safe to leave the cat in the flight overnight to catch the unwanted visitors.

Keeping cats at bay

A cat is useful to the birdkeeper not only to deter rodents, but also because, with its strongly territorial nature, it will keep other cats out of the garden. You may find, however,

Below: *A garden shed, such as this one, makes an ideal birdroom, providing space for both indoor flights and storage.*

that a cat becomes a major problem. Some will persist in climbing onto the aviary, disturbing the parakeets, even if not harming them directly. Losses of recently fledged young are often the result of the parakeets flying hard at the aviary mesh as they try to escape from an unwelcome cat.

You can protect the aviary against cats by putting a false roof on top of the aviary flight. Build the structure, which should be at least 22.5cm(9in) high, from 22-gauge, 5cm(2in) square mesh attached to a thin, 2.5cm(1in)-square, wooden frame. The gaps in the mesh will be wide enough to deter cats.

Introducing birds to the aviary
It can be helpful to shut newly purchased parakeets in the shelter for a day or two before letting them into the flight. As they are likely to be nervous at first, make sure that you have everything prepared in advance, and leave them to settle quietly in their quarters. They will soon adjust to the change in their environment and become used to feeding in the shelter.

If you want to keep the parakeets on a colony system, it is important to wait until you have assembled all members of the group before releasing them all into the aviary together. Otherwise, any newcomers introduced at a later date are likely to be persecuted by the established birds.

Always watch the parakeets closely after you have moved them, as problems are most likely to arise at this stage. You should also keep an eye on birds that have been transferred to the aviary from indoor winter accommodation. The parakeets may bathe so enthusiastically in the first shower of rain that they become waterlogged and temporarily unable to fly. You can give parakeets the equivalent of a bath by regularly spraying them while they are housed indoors. Use a plant sprayer, directing the jet over the parakeet's head so that water falls on it from above rather than hitting it directly.

Catching aviary parakeets
Since many parakeets are very quick in flight, they can be difficult to catch in aviary surroundings. Remove the perches from the flight to give you easier access to all corners, then shut off the shelter to keep the birds in the flight. A deep catching net, that is well-padded around the edges, provides the simplest means of catching parakeets, and the padded rim will help to protect them from injury.

You will probably find it easier to catch the birds in the net when they are resting on the aviary mesh, rather than in flight. Once the parakeet is inside the net, place one hand over the opening to stop the bird slipping out again, and gently lower the net to the ground. Then, with the same hand, reach in and hold the bird gently. It is advisable to have a thin pair of gloves available; parakeets can give a painful nip, and those with larger beaks, such as the Alexandrine, may even draw blood. Hold the bird so that its head rests between the first and second fingers of your hand, and its wings are restrained against your palm. Be very careful not to exert any pressure with your fingers around the parakeet's neck.

As you draw the parakeet out of the net, you will probably find that it has clenched its feet into the material of the net. Using your other hand, you will need to prize the claws gently away from the net to free the bird. You can inspect its body easily while it is in this position in your hand if you wish. Otherwise, place it straight into a secure box from which it cannot escape (see page 13).

You may have difficulty in catching the parakeets, but try not to stress them unduly. Watch their breathing; if they show clear signs of gasping with an open mouth, leave them quietly for a few minutes to recover before trying again. If the weather is hot, catch the birds either in the early morning or in the evening, when the temperature is likely to be cooler than during the daytime.

Feeding parakeets

Parakeets are generally easy birds to cater for, requiring a diet comprised largely of seeds, nuts, greenstuff and fruit. Most will not eat invertebrates of any kind, although kakarikis have been known to take mealworms regularly, especially during the breeding season.

One of the main reasons why Australian species adapted so well to aviculture, at a time when little was known about the nutritional needs of parrots in general, was their ability to breed on a diet of dry seed and water. Nowadays, there are a number of specially developed pellets and impregnated seeds for parakeets. These foodstuffs have been partially responsible for the great improvement, during recent years, in the breeding performance of parakeets from other continents.

Seeds and nuts

The seeds used for feeding parakeets can be divided into the grass seeds, which in their cultivated forms are known as cereals, and the oil seeds, especially sunflower.

Canary seed and millet are the major cereals of significance as bird food, and can be easily distinguished by their shape; canary seed is oval with pointed ends, whereas millet is round.

You will see a number of different types of millet in parakeet seed mixtures, including the large pearl white seeds and red millet. Probably the most popular types of millet for parakeets are panicum and Japanese millet. You can buy panicum either as loose seed, or in the form of sprays (the seedheads) – a favourite with parakeets.

The different crops of canary seed grown throughout the world are less distinctive, but are nevertheless sold on the basis of their country of origin, usually Canada or Morocco. The nutritional value of seed is related directly to its growing conditions. As deficiencies may occur in seeds from certain localities, it is a good idea to offer a mix to the parakeets.

There are several types of sunflower seed, grown mostly in the warmer parts of the world. The striped form is the one most commonly used as bird food, but the large seeds, in particular, tend to be comprised largely of husk, which the birds discard, and have only a small kernel. Because sunflower is the major ingredient of margarine and other oils used by the food industry, its oil content is often developed to the detriment of its protein value. White sunflower seed is more suitable as bird food than striped or black forms, because it has a higher level of protein, but the yield per hectare is lower, which makes it more costly. It is therefore not usually included in any quantity in seed mixtures. You can purchase it separately, however, and add it to the parakeets' regular diet.

Another popular seed with many parakeets is safflower seed. At first glance, these seeds may be confused with white sunflower, but they are, in fact, smaller and more round in shape.

Not all the seeds used for parakeets are cultivated – pine nuts are collected from the wild especially for this purpose. They are readily consumed by parakeets, particularly by psittaculid species, which eat such seeds in their natural habitat. During recent years, a smaller grade of pine nut from China has appeared on the market. These seeds are ideal for the smaller species, such as *Bolborhynchus* parakeets, which may encounter difficulty in cracking the larger pine nuts. You can also offer a number of other nuts, such as walnuts and brazils, to Alexandrines and other similarly sized species, but you will probably need to crack the harder shell of these nuts for them.

Peanuts, also known as monkey nuts when they are enclosed in their wafer-like shells, are commonly added to many parakeet seed mixes. They are not recommended for grass parakeets and similar species, however, because they are less digestible

than sunflower, though equally fattening. Incidentally, you should never feed salted nuts of any kind as a treat for a parakeet, as they could kill the bird.

Certain seeds are used more commonly at particular times of the year. Hemp, a dark, roundish seed and one of the oil-based seed group, is favoured as a source of energy during the colder months of the year. It is a favourite with most parakeets, but you should limit the amount you offer, as excessive quantities will lead to obesity. Groats, (which are dehusked oats), are popular as a rearing food during the breeding season, but you can also add this cereal to the seed mixture throughout the year.

As a general rule, Australian species need a much higher intake

Above: Millet sprays are popular with all parakeets, especially Australian species, such as this Elegant. Soaked millet is widely used in rearing diets.

of cereal seeds than parakeets from other continents. Rather than mixing your own blend of seed, you can buy special packeted mixes from your pet shop. For most Australian species, choose a cockatiel or budgerigar seed mixture and add a little sunflower.

The Asiatic and American parakeets will prefer a parrot seed mixture, comprised largely of sunflower, peanuts and possibly hemp and safflower. To this, you should add pine nuts and some of the other seeds mentioned above. Larger species, such as the

Alexandrine, generally show less inclination to sample the smaller cereal seeds, but some, such as the Plum-headed Parakeet, often show a marked preference for these seeds.

As birds differ in their individual tastes, you should offer a reasonably wide variety of seed. It is a good idea to provide cereals in a separate container, since, because of their size, they tend to sink to the bottom, where they become lost in the surrounding chaff, if they are added to a parrot seed mixture.

Buying and storing seed
It is important that you check that the seed you are buying is clean. If it is in a plastic bag, hold it up so that you can look at the bottom, where dirt usually accumulates along with fodder mites – minute pests, just visible to the naked eye. These mites attack seed, although it is not certain that they cause any direct harm to the birds. If they are present in large numbers, they will give the seed a rather sweet and sickly smell, especially if it has been stored for a time.

Seed that contains mouse droppings is definitely more harmful, and various diseases can be spread to parakeets in this way. Thankfully, such occurrences are rare, as most seed is carefully harvested and stored.

Look out for any signs of green mould on pine nuts. This tends to be most common on chipped, damaged nuts, and could obviously prove a threat to the parakeets' health. Similarly, mouldy peanuts are dangerous, producing aflatoxins, which can have serious effects on the parakeet's liver.

If you keep seed and nuts in a dry environment after purchase, such problems are unlikely to arise. Always store seed in metal bins, not only to keep it dry, but also so that it is out of the reach of rodents. This is one of the simplest means of excluding these pests from the aviary. Seed that has been left around in bags will often prove an irresistible target for them.

Above: *Carrot is a valuable source of Vitamin A. Having washed and peeled it, you can either grate it, or offer a piece whole, as here.*

Pellets
Research into the dietary needs of parakeets has led to the marketing of pelleted foods, which should offer a more balanced diet than seed alone. The problem has been to persuade the birds to take pellets as readily as seed, but, with perseverance, you should be able to coax most parakeets to sample them. Start by adding the pellets along with the seed; if necessary, reducing the amount of seed on offer to encourage the birds to try the pellets.

You can introduce young parakeets to pellets as part of their regular diet as soon as they become independent, when their natural curiosity should make it much easier for you to persuade them to take this food. Do not be surprised if the water consumption of the parakeets increases as they start eating pellets. This is a normal reaction to the dry nature of the pellets. You may need to provide an additional drinker to ensure that an adequate water supply is constantly available.

Fruit and greenfood
In the wild, parakeets feed on fruit and greenfood, such as buds and

shoots, and you should offer fresh supplies regularly to pet and aviary birds. Sweet apple is universally popular, and available throughout the year, whereas other fruits tend to be more seasonal. Pomegranates, however, can be stored successfully for several months and will be greedily taken by South American parakeets, in particular. The *Brotogeris* species appear to need more fruit in their regular diet than other parakeets.

Australian species often show a marked preference for greenstuff, such as chickweed (*Stellaria media*) or seeding grasses. Chickweed is easy to grow throughout much of the year in a shaded, damp patch of earth. (If it is exposed to excessive sunlight, it loses its leafy appearance and becomes rather straggling in its growth.) You can obtain chickweed seed from a horticultural supplier specializing in wild plants.

As an alternative to chickweed, you can grow perpetual spinach. You will be able to feed this fresh throughout the year as it thrives under a variety of soil conditions. Its thick stems are popular with psittaculid parakeets, in particular.

Always wash all greenfood and fruit before offering it to the parakeets, in case it has been soiled by wild animals or birds. You can also deep-freeze some fresh foods for use during the winter. Grapes, for example, will freeze well. Place them loose on trays in the freezer and, when they are frozen, tip them into clean, plastic boxes for storage. You will then be able to remove the grapes from the freezer in small quantities for feeding to the parakeets.

Corn-on-the-cob is also suitable for freezing, although you will need to blanch it first. After defrosting, cook in the normal way and allow to cool before offering it to the parakeets. South American and psittaculid species are particularly fond of this vegetable.

Like corn-on-the-cob, carrots are a good source of Vitamin A. Wash, peel, and cut up the carrots into small pieces. This helps to prevent wastage, as smaller pieces are less likely to be spilt and food that falls on the floor tends to be ignored by the parakeets.

You can also use fresh food as a means of dispensing a food supplement. Powder supplements tend to be more comprehensive in terms of their ingredients than

What to feed your parakeet		
Group	**Seed**	**Fruit and greenstuff**
Grass parakeets Bolborhynchus parakeets	Canary seed and millets.	Offer a daily selection of sweet apple, chick-weed and seeding grasses.
Larger Australian parakeets	Canary seed, millets, sunflower seeds, groats and small pine nuts.	As above.
Psittaculid parakeets	Parrot mix of sunflower seeds, peanuts, pine nuts and pumpkin seeds. Feed smaller species on seed and millet.	Provide a daily selection of sweet apple, grapes and other fruit, carrot, perpetual spinach and chickweed.
Brotogeris parakeets	Parrot seeds, especially the smaller types, such as groats and safflower.	Offer sweet apple, grapes, banana and other fruit daily.

liquid forms. Simply sprinkle the required amount of powder over the damp surface of the greenstuff, fruit or vegetables. Seed is far less effective for this purpose, because the parakeets dehusk the seed and so any supplement on the husk will be wasted. As a way round this problem, however, some manufacturers offer impregnated seed, notably canary seed and millets, which have the supplement added to the kernel. This is a useful addition to the parakeets' diet, especially if the birds are reluctant to take fresh food.

Grit and minerals
Parakeets use their beaks to crack seeds and, if necessary, to gnaw their food into pieces sufficiently small for them to swallow easily. Under normal circumstances, food passes into the crop before continuing through to the proventriculus and then the gizzard, where the digestive process begins in earnest.

Grit fulfills several functions. Firstly, it helps to prevent the seed from forming lumpy aggregates by breaking it down into smaller pieces on which the digestive enzymes can work effectively. The walls of the gizzard in a seed-eating bird, such as a parakeet, are very muscular, assisting this grinding process. Furthermore, as the grit itself breaks down, it releases valuable minerals, which are absorbed into the bird's body.

It is useful to mix oystershell grit and mineralized grit to improve the bird's intake of minerals, and of vital trace elements, such as iodine, which are needed in smaller amounts. Packets of both sorts of grit are available from pet shops. Provide grit in a separate container from seed, and fill up the pot each week, so the parakeets have a regular supply.

Calcium is a vital ingredient of eggshells and parakeets will consume great quantities of this mineral at the start of the breeding period. A deficiency will lead to soft-shelled eggs, and possibly other complications, such as egg-

Above: *Provide seed mixtures in containers that are easy to clean. This particular type can be hooked onto the aviary mesh.*

binding (see page 43). You should offer calcium either in the form of cuttlefish bone or as a special block, both of which are available from most pet shops.

Calcium blocks are supplied with a wire tape, which simply needs to be twisted around the aviary mesh to hold the block in place. You can buy special clips to attach cuttlefish bones to the cage or aviary mesh, or simply use wire to fix them firmly in place. Choose a spot close to a perch so that the parakeets can reach the bone easily.

Food and drink containers
There are some designs of seed hopper available that are suitable for dispensing sunflower seeds and similar large nuts, but the majority, being intended for use with budgerigars, are only large enough for millet and canary seed. You will need a hopper that operates on an open-flow basis, rather than one with holes, which are too small for many parakeets, and will prevent the birds reaching the seed.

Alternatively, offer seed in open containers. Use earthenware pots, as sold for dogs, placed on the floor for Australian species, or hook special containers onto the mesh lining the shelter. Position these near a perch, so that spillage is kept to a minimum.

Plastic containers are suitable for many species, but for more destructive parakeets you may decide to use the metal feeders. You will need to file away any sharp pieces of metal around the edges of the pot, otherwise they may injure a parakeet's foot.

If you are keeping parakeets in groups, offer a choice of feeding sites. This is particularly recommended for certain psittaculid parakeets, especially if the hen proves very dominant outside the breeding period, as she may actually prevent the cock bird from eating if there is only one feeder available. Remove as much husk from the top of the container as possible before placing fresh seed on top each day, and empty out the pot completely and wash it every week or so. Ensure that the container is completely dry before refilling it, otherwise the moisture may cause the seed to start germinating and turn mouldy.

Drinking water for parakeets is usually supplied in tubular drinkers or bottles, which hook onto the sides of the aviary by means of a special clip or metal loop. These sealed containers help to ensure that the water remains fresh and uncontaminated by dirt or faecal matter. As with food, the drinking water should be available in the

Below: *A tubular drinker should ensure that the birds have a supply of clean water available.*

shelter, rather than in the flight. Exposed to bright light, drinkers soon become covered with algal growth. They are also more likely to be split outdoors, as the water freezes in cold weather. Always leave a slight gap when filling the drinker in freezing temperatures, to allow for expansion of the water.

Change the water every day, to ensure the parakeets always have fresh uncontaminated drinking water, and wash the containers at least once a week. If you add any liquid supplements to the drinking water, always rinse the container thoroughly afterwards. Do not use metal drinkers of any kind if you are administering medicine in the drinking water, as the medicine could react with the metal.

You can clean both food and drink containers with a range of brushes (special bottle brushes are sold for tubular drinkers and food hoppers) and a safe disinfectant.

Soaked seed

Soaked seed makes a welcome addition to the parakeets' diet, especially during the breeding season. You can prepare canary seed, millets (including sprays) and even sunflower in this fashion, simply by covering a small amount of seed with hot water, leaving to stand for a day, and then rinsing the seed very thoroughly under a running tap. After draining off the surplus water, transfer the seed to a clean container.

The advantages in offering soaked seed are, firstly, that it is more digestible, and therefore of particular value when there are chicks in the nest, and, secondly, that its protein level is increased. However, once seed has been soaked, it becomes perishable foodstuff and you will need to remove any that is not eaten before it starts to turn mouldy. Breeders in hot countries therefore usually prefer not to use soaked seed. Most birds will take soaked seed very readily, so you only need to leave it in the feeders for a few hours. Wash containers used for soaked seed immediately after use.

Basic health care

Parakeets are normally very healthy birds, and there is probably more likelihood that you will encounter injuries than illness in your stock. Few birds are easier to look after than parakeets, but they will need attention every day. Although you can provide them with plenty of food and water, sufficient to last several days, you should, nevertheless, check them at least twice every day, in the morning and late afternoon, to ensure that they have not fallen ill or injured themselves. Injuries are especially likely to occur if the birds are disturbed after dark, which causes them to fly wildly around the aviary. They may sustain superficial cuts, or worse, a brain haemorrhage, which is rapidly fatal. Australian species are the most vulnerable, partly because they are more nervous by nature, but also because they appear to have thinner skulls.

Physical injuries
If you find a parakeet on the floor of the aviary looking dazed, examine its head closely to try to discover the point of impact. There is really nothing that you can do, however, apart from moving the bird to a quiet, darkened environment in the hope that it will recover. A box lined with paper towelling is ideal, but leave it in a secure place, away from cats and other animals that might disturb it. Hopefully, the parakeet will be showing signs of recovery within a few hours.

There is usually no need to worry about minor bleeding, as clotting takes place rapidly. But if bleeding is more severe, perhaps resulting from a torn claw, you may need a styptic pencil, or a solution of cold potash alum, to stem the blood loss. Apply the alum on cotton wool, pressing it tightly on the cut end of the claw. The bleeding should stop within minutes.

Try to discover the cause of any injury by inspecting the bird and the aviary. It may be that the parakeet's claws were too long, and had started to curl round at an abnormal angle, so that the bird

became caught up in the mesh and was unable to free itself.

Under normal circumstances, the claws rarely need trimming, but it is usually an easy task to carry out when necessary. Use a pair of nail-cutters rather than scissors, which tend to split the nail instead of cutting through it cleanly. Hold the parakeet in a good light, so that you can find the blood supply, which extends for a short distance down each claw. You will need to cut towards the tip of the claw, below the vessel, to avoid bleeding. (Similarly, you will need to locate the blood supply to the bird's beak, should you ever need to trim it.)

Frostbite is another, less obvious cause of bleeding, and may occur if parakeets have roosted out in the open part of the aviary. The first signs you are likely to find are traces of blood on the perches. If you then closely inspect the parakeets themselves, you will notice that they are reluctant to use their injured toes, which will appear rather red and swollen.

Unfortunately, there is little that you can do once the damage is done, although massaging the damaged toes or holding them in warm water may help. If the injury is severe, the blood, and thus the oxygen, supply to the extremities will be lost, causing the affected toe to shrivel up over the course of ten days or so and ultimately drop off. Depending on the number of digits affected, the parakeet may have difficulty in perching.

Some species, notably the Long-tailed Parakeet, appear especially susceptible to frostbite. Always ensure that such birds are adequately protected during periods of cold weather, even if otherwise they are properly acclimatized. They may use a nestbox for roosting purposes, but if not, you will need to shut them in the shelter each evening before dusk during cold weather.

Infectious diseases
Parakeets can succumb to various infections, but if they are properly fed and established in clean

Above: *A bird's claws sometimes become overgrown and you will need to trim them with a stout pair of clippers. Be sure to locate the blood supply before cutting.*

surroundings, you are unlikely to encounter such problems. A much publicized, but uncommon, disease is psittacosis, now more accurately called chlamydiosis. It is an important disease because humans have been known to contract the infection from birds. In man, the symptoms are respiratory problems, which, on rare occasions, may prove fatal, although with antibiotic treatment this is highly unlikely. Nevertheless, a long period of convalescence may be necessary. The likelihood of encountering the disease is slight, but as the symptoms in parakeets are not specific, you should treat newly acquired birds that fall sick with caution. Always seek advice from your veterinarian, who will, if necessary, carry out tests to give a definite diagnosis.

Some diseases are more common at certain times of the year. Pseudotuberculosis, for example, so-named because it resembles avian tuberculosis, is more likely to be encountered during damp spells in the winter, rather than in the summer. It can

also be spread by rodents. Pseudotuberculosis is invariably fatal, with death either occuring suddenly, or following a week or so of weight loss and inappetence. Regular cleaning and disinfection of the aviary will prevent the build-up of such diseases.

Antibiotics can effectively counter many of the bacterial illnesses that parakeets may contract, provided that you begin treatment at an early stage of the infection.

It is worthwhile having an infrared heat lamp and a cage specifically for sick birds, especially if you have a large collection. Choose a lamp that emits heat, rather than light, so that the parakeet will not suffer under the bright glare. By keeping the bird warm, you will conserve its body temperature, which should allow the medication to work more effectively.

The easiest means of administering medication to the birds is to dissolve the antibiotic powder in the drinking water. You will need to change this solution twice daily. You can also offer canary seed impregnated with an antibiotic, but as many sick parakeets lose their appetite, this may not be satisfactory. Your veterinarian will advise you.

The drug can also be injected,

Above: *Use an infrared lamp –
choose one that emits heat rather
than light – to keep a sick bird
warm. Position it as here, or
suspend it above an all-wire cage.*

usually in critical cases, or, for the
larger parakeets, administered in
tablet form. Place the tablet as far
back in the mouth as possible, and
hold the beak shut for a few
moments to encourage the bird to
swallow the medication. Although
they can be more stressful for the
bird, these direct methods tend to
be more effective than applying the
powdered drug to fruit or water,
because a known amount of the
drug is taken. However you
administer medication, be sure to
follow the dosage instructions
carefully. Most sick birds undergo
an apparently rapid recovery when
they receive effective treatment,
but you must always complete the
course of antibiotics, otherwise a
relapse may occur.

As the sick bird recovers, slowly
reduce the temperature in the cage
to reacclimatize the parakeet
before replacing it in the aviary. If it
is winter, you may need to keep the

bird indoors until the following
spring. Be sure to disinfect the
cage and all utensils thoroughly,
and dry them out so that they are
ready for use again when required.

If you lose a bird, it is always
worthwhile having a post-mortem
examination carried out to establish
the cause of death. This may save
others in your collection, if you give
them appropriate medication
without delay.

Parasitic infestations
Parakeets are potentially at risk
from a variety of parasitic
infestations, but by careful
monitoring of new stock you should
be able to avoid such problems.
Parasites can be broadly divided
into two categories, those living
outside the body, on the feathers
and skin of the parakeet, and those
found internally.

Scaly face, caused by
Cnemidocoptes mites, results in
growths resembling coral and is
thought to spread from adults to
nestlings by direct contact.
However, the mites appear to be
able to survive away from living
organisms; kakarikis transferred to

accommodation where infected budgerigars were previously housed subsequently developed scaly face. Administer a proprietary remedy at the first sign of the disease – snail-like tracks across the upper beak. If you delay treatment, malformation of the beak may result. The mites can also infest the feet, giving rise to scaly feet, and even the rest of the body.

Wash the birds' quarters thoroughly with an effective disinfectant once treatment is completed. It is also a good idea to change the perches, where the mites may be hidden.

Red mite is a particular danger during the breeding period. A heavy infestation in a nestbox can result in anaemic chicks and may trigger feather-plucking because of the irritation caused by the mites.

It is possible that wild birds, such as sparrows, may spread red mites to aviary occupants. Although these parasites are usually in close contact with the birds, they rarely live permanently on them. You will need to take regular precautions against these parasites by spraying all newly acquired birds with a specially formulated avian aerosol intended to kill mites.

You should also wash nestboxes thoroughly at the end of each breeding season using one of the preparations marketed for this purpose. It is a wise precaution to give the parakeets' quarters a good clean at the same time.

Although many parakeets appear to be infested, the danger of illness associated with these particular parasites is generally unclear. Some apparently have no ill effects on the bird, but there is evidence to show that red mites are responsible for transmitting some microscopic blood parasites, which may cause avian malaria.

The *Leucocytozoon* parasite is similar, but is spread by flies that breed in stagnant water, rather than by mites. Infestations most commonly arise in aviary stock housed close to standing water, such as ponds. There are few signs prior to death, which results from heart failure. A post-mortem examination should reveal the parasites encysted in the heart muscle. Outbreaks of this disease have led to losses in various collections, notably in the south of England, although fatalities have been recorded elsewhere.

If you live in an area where this disease is known to occur, probably the only satisfactory solution will be to cover the aviary with mosquito netting to prevent the flies gaining access to the birds. Preventive medication may also be a good idea, especially if you cannot drain the water where the flies are breeding.

Intestinal worms in parakeets are virtually universal and can cause a wide variety of symptoms, ranging from malaise to death. Roundworms are the major threat because of their direct life cycles. The eggs are infective a short time after they have been passed out of the parakeet's body, because they do not need to spend part of their life cycle in a different host. Food or water containers that are contaminated with droppings provide an easy means of spreading these parasites.

Tapeworms rarely pose a serious threat because of their indirect life cycles. These flat worms are attached to the gut, and segments containing their eggs are voided in the droppings. The eggs are not a direct hazard to the parakeet and the bird will not be infected unless it eats an invertebrate, such as a snail, that has consumed the tapeworm eggs. Occasionally, birds may eat an infected insect, on a piece of fruit, for example, and tapeworm infestations have been recorded in *Brotogeris* parakeets.

The presence of worm eggs in the birds' droppings can be ascertained by a relatively simple and inexpensive procedure, which can identify the different parasites accurately by the shape of their eggs. Besides being of diagnostic value, the test will also help to monitor the progress of treatment. Your veterinarian will be able to advise on testing and provide you

Life cycles of parasites

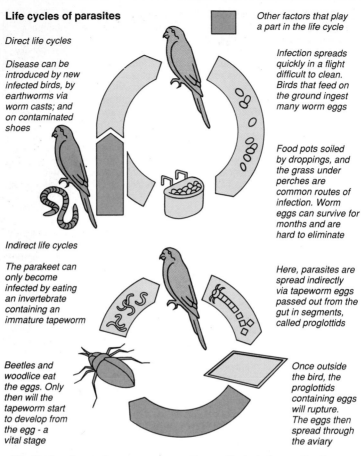

Direct life cycles

Disease can be introduced by new infected birds, by earthworms via worm casts; and on contaminated shoes

Other factors that play a part in the life cycle

Infection spreads quickly in a flight difficult to clean. Birds that feed on the ground ingest many worm eggs

Food pots soiled by droppings, and the grass under perches are common routes of infection. Worm eggs can survive for months and are hard to eliminate

Indirect life cycles

The parakeet can only become infected by eating an invertebrate containing an immature tapeworm

Here, parasites are spread indirectly via tapeworm eggs passed out from the gut in segments, called proglottids

Beetles and woodlice eat the eggs. Only then will the tapeworm start to develop from the egg - a vital stage

Once outside the bird, the proglottids containing eggs will rupture. The eggs then spread through the aviary

with effective deworming medication. This will prove more satisfactory if you treat each parakeet individually, rather than simply adding the drug to the drinking water. Dewormers are generally bitter, and the parakeets will be able to detect this, in spite of their rather limited sense of taste. It is also worthwhile keeping the parakeets caged for a short time until the effects of the drug have worn off. You will be able to see the worms on the floor of the cage.

Australian parakeets are commonly infested with parasitic worms, probably because they spend more time on the ground, where the greatest concentration of worm eggs are found. The worms produce many thousands of eggs in a short space of time, so, as well as

Above: *Control of parasitic disease depends upon breaking the life cycle. Roundworms present the greatest threat because they are easily spread from bird to bird.*

treating the birds themselves, do not forget to clean their surroundings thoroughly.

If you suspect that a parakeet is suffering from a particularly bad infestation, offer a little olive oil at the same time as dosing with the vermifuge. The gut of a parakeet narrows as it progresses through to the cloaca and, clearly, dislodging a knot of worms high up the tract could lead to a fatal blockage lower down. The olive oil will act as a laxative to lessen this risk.

When administering fluids of any kind to a parakeet, do be careful to

avoid the windpipe, which is evident as an opening at the back of the mouth. Obviously, if fluid enters here accidentally, the parakeet may choke. For this reason, experienced parakeet-keepers often choose to medicate their birds using a tube, which they pass down the throat into the crop. Do not undertake this process without seeking proper advice and assistance, however, or you may damage the bird.

Although, of course, it is always better to eliminate the parasites before they gain a hold in your aviary, regular preventive deworming is standard practice with most birdkeepers. Ideally, you should treat the birds twice a year, giving the first dose just before the onset of the breeding season.

Egg-binding

You are only likely to encounter this serious ailment in mature hens, usually those using a nestbox. Psittaculid parakeets are possibly most at risk, as Ringnecks, for example, often lay earlier than other species, when the weather may still be quite cold.

Chilling, which slows muscular activity, and a lack of calcium, which causes soft-shelled eggs, are probably the two most significant causes of egg-binding. The affected hen will be unable to lay the egg in the normal way, and it will remain trapped in her body.

The first visible sign of egg-binding is that the hen will appear unsteady on her feet. Soon she will

Above: *Individual dosing of a bird provides the most effective treatment against parasitic worms.*

be unable to perch, as the trapped egg causes pressure on nerve endings, and her condition will rapidly deteriorate unless you manage to remove the egg.

Take particular care when catching a hen that you suspect is suffering in this way. If the egg ruptures inside her body, it may cause peritonitis (a severe infection of the body cavity). Transfer her to a warm place, where the temperature is about 32°C(90°F). The most effective means of treatment is an injection of a calcium compound, administered by a veterinarian. If this fails, there is a possibility of removing the egg by surgery. In any event, the hen must be allowed to recover on her own, and you should not use her again for breeding purposes for at least another year.

A complication that may occasionally arise from egg-binding is a prolapse of the lower part of the oviduct. The prolapse results from prolonged straining, and shows as pinkish tissue protruding from the vent. It must be replaced without delay, and can be dabbed with a non-toxic germicidal ointment. If the problem persists, your veterinarian will insert a special suture around the vent to stop the prolapse reappearing. Within a few days, muscle tone will have been restored, and the suture can be safely removed.

Breeding and rearing parakeets

Parakeets vary in their breeding requirements and habits. Some species, such as the grass parakeets, are happy to breed in an aviary of fairly modest dimensions, whereas others, such as Crimsonwings, generally do better in more spacious surroundings. Most parakeets need to be kept on their own in individual pairs, especially during the breeding season, but you should buy a small group of *Brotogeris* parakeets, as these birds appear to need the company of others of their kind to stimulate breeding activity. Similarly, other South American species, such as the Quaker Parakeet and *Bolborhynchus* species, often breed more successfully when kept in groups.

Certain parakeet species will prove quite prolific – many Australian parakeets nest twice during the warmer part of the year. In contrast, New World parakeets rarely rear more than one round of chicks each year in outside aviaries. Certainly, you will find the latter more challenging, as they are also less keen to reproduce than their Australian counterparts.

Although their aviary requirements and breeding habits differ, the care you will need to give the pair and their chicks remains fairly constant for all species. Here, we look at suitable diets and nestboxes for the breeding birds, and how to hand feed and rear the chicks, if necessary, until they are independent.

Feeding breeding birds
Unless parakeets are properly fed, as well as suitably housed, they will be unwilling to start nesting. Prior to the onset of the breeding period, you may want to increase the protein level of their diet, as this helps to stimulate breeding condition. Some manufacturers of pelleted diets produce both a maintenance ration and a breeding diet, and you can simply change from one to the other as appropriate. (The pellets of both diets look the same but their ingredients vary slightly.)

Mineral intake is particularly important for hens during the breeding season, and you will find that you need to replace cuttlefish bone frequently as the time for laying approaches. This is one of the first signs that the birds are ready to start nesting in earnest. Some breeders, especially in continental Europe, also offer rock salt, to Australian parakeets in particular. Rock salt, which is available from many large supermarkets, contains various trace elements, such as iodine, that may stimulate breeding behaviour.

Nestboxes
The basic design of the nestbox does not vary greatly but, clearly, the size will differ depending on the species. A fairly deep nestbox is preferred by most parakeets, especially larger Australian species and the psittaculids, as it appears to offer them a greater degree of

Below: *Some species, especially Crimsonwings and king parakeets (shown here), prefer a deep 'grandfather clock' nestbox, which appears to offer greater security.*

security. You can buy nestboxes either complete or in kit form for home assembly. The timber or plywood used for their construction will be at least 1.25cm(0.5in) thick (and preferably double this). Wood is a good insulator and the birds will be reasonably warm inside the box, even in cold weather. Warmth is particularly important for the youngsters of the Plum-headed Parakeet, as the adults cease to brood the chicks at night before they are fully feathered. A robustly constructed nestbox will be less easily destroyed by the parakeets' beaks, and therefore less dangerous to their eggs and chicks.

If you choose to make the nestbox yourself, attach a simple ladder on the inside of the box, to run down from the entrance hole to near the base. You can use aviary mesh for this ladder, but take care not to leave any loose, sharp ends of mesh. Cutting down one side of the roll will give you one smooth edge, but you will need to file back any projections on the other edge and on the top and bottom of the ladder. You can give further protection to the edges by tacking thin battening to them, although the parakeets are likely to gnaw this away in time. Fix the mesh ladder firmly in place with netting staples down each side and along the top and bottom. (If the parakeets are able to dislodge the ladder, they could be trapped in the nestbox.)

A typical parakeet nestbox

Below: *This nestbox, 30cm(12in) wide and deep, and 45cm(18in) tall, is suitable for most parakeets.*

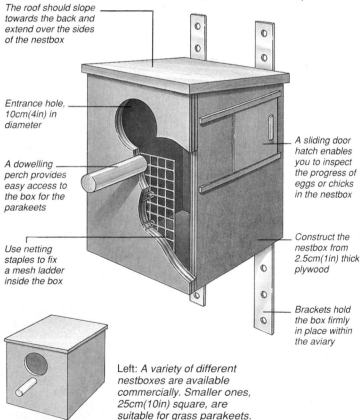

The roof should slope towards the back and extend over the sides of the nestbox

Entrance hole, 10cm(4in) in diameter

A dowelling perch provides easy access to the box for the parakeets

Use netting staples to fix a mesh ladder inside the box

A sliding door hatch enables you to inspect the progress of eggs or chicks in the nestbox

Construct the nestbox from 2.5cm(1in) thick plywood

Brackets hold the box firmly in place within the aviary

Left: *A variety of different nestboxes are available commercially. Smaller ones, 25cm(10in) square, are suitable for grass parakeets.*

Using a jigsaw, cut an entrance hole near the top of the front of the box, and a smaller one just below it, into which you can fit a perch on the outside of the box. It is also important that you have easy access to the nestbox. Bear in mind that once the box is fixed near the top of the aviary, it will be difficult for you to open the lid to look inside. It is therefore worthwhile cutting another access hole on one of the sides. Position this high enough for it to be out of the birds' reach while they are nesting in the base of the box, otherwise they will attack this opening. The door covering this access should be a sliding one, rather than one hinged to open downwards, which might open accidentally.

The roof should just overlap the sides, so that if the nestbox becomes wet, the water will drain off, rather than running onto the box. Never cover the roof with felt, which the parakeets will chew and which may be toxic. Ideally, however, you should position the nestbox in a sheltered, dry spot in the covered area of the flight.

Secure supports will be necessary to hold the nestbox in place and should be positioned underneath the box, if possible. Brackets offer the simplest means of fixing the nestbox to the aviary. Use screws, which you can easily remove at the end of the breeding season, to hold it in place.

Some parakeets will use their nestbox as a roosting site at night, and this is obviously to be encouraged on a winter evening. If possible, however, transfer the box into the shelter during the winter period and move it outside again (after washing it thoroughly) in the early spring. If you do not return it soon enough, the parakeets may lay their eggs in a seed pot or even directly onto the floor. Most Australian species will only use their nestbox during the breeding season and, since its presence may encourage them to lay during the winter, you should remove it from the aviary in the autumn.

Above: *An all-mesh indoor breeding cage. It is quite possible to breed parakeets in such surroundings, but avoid any unnecessary disturbances.*

Above: *Avoid interfering with the chicks if all appears to be going well. Some pairs will be very intolerant of nest inspection.*

Above: *These young Cobalt-winged Parakeets are the chicks of the adult birds shown at top and centre and are just three days old.*

The birds will require some time to prepare the nest before starting to lay. A satisfactory floor covering in the nestbox is essential. Most species prefer to make their own nest lining by gnawing up short lengths of softwood battening placed inside the nestbox. As an alternative, you can use coarse wood shavings, sold by pet shops for small animal bedding. Avoid sawdust, however, which tends to create too much dust. Although peat is sometimes recommended as a nest lining, many parakeets appear to dislike this material and will scratch it out of the nestbox. And again, once it is dry, it becomes very dusty.

The breeding period

Try to leave the pair undisturbed as much as possible, especially if they have not bred before. One of the most reliable indicators that all is going well is an increase in the food consumption of the parakeets; feeding times assume great importance throughout the breeding season. If you make a point of feeding the birds at the same time each day – which is always recommended – you will probably find that the hen will emerge to take some favoured fresh item, such as fruit or greenfood. While the hen is out of the nestbox, you may be able to look inside for a brief moment.

Before she begins to lay, the hen will start to spend more time in the nestbox during the day. She may appear nervous, coming out at the slightest sound, but this need not cause you concern. Following the laying of the second or third egg of the clutch, she will start to incubate seriously. Although cock parakeets take no direct part in this activity, they may join their mate in the nestbox for intervals during the day, as well as at night.

By careful observation, you should have an idea of when the hen laid and the most likely date that the chicks will hatch. Just prior to laying, the hen's droppings will have a very pungent odour and become noticeably larger in size. Again, this is not a cause for concern and they will return to normal after she has laid.

Below: *Note the crop of these young Ring-necked Parakeets, which is visible as a swelling at the base of the neck. The developing feather tracts can also be seen.*

It is important not to disturb a sitting hen; if she is forced out of the nestbox, she may scatter, and thus damage, the eggs. Young chicks, too, may be injured, or even dragged out of the nestbox.

Hand-rearing
The first few days after hatching are fairly critical in the life of the chicks. Although the majority of parakeets make good parents, a few, perhaps most notably Alexandrine Parakeets, can be poor feeders, and the chicks will be lost unless you remove and hand feed them. This problem is most likely to arise with young hens that are breeding for the first time, but it can become habitual.

You should obtain all the necessary items for hand-feeding before the start of the breeding season so that, in an emergency, you can feed the chicks without delay. The special balanced hand-rearing diets now available are preferable to other formulations

Below: *Hand-feeding a young chick using a spoon with its edges bent to form a funnel. Special hand-rearing diets are now produced.*

that are generally based around human infant foods.

Newly hatched chicks will need a fairly liquid food for the first day or so. Mix the food with hot water, checking the temperature on the back of your hand before feeding the chicks. If it is too hot, it will scald their mouths, while cold food will tend to slow down the whole digestive process, and the food will remain in the young chicks' crop for longer than usual.

The crop, which is a sac-like structure located at the base of the neck, is clearly evident in young chicks and provides the best means of monitoring their food intake. Allow the young parakeets to feed at their own pace. The safest way of feeding them is to use a teaspoon with the edges carefully bent in to form a channel. The chick's crop will appear reasonably full when the bird has eaten enough and will gradually empty between feeds. Initially, the chicks will need to be fed every two hours or so. Keep the chicks as clean as possible, and always wipe their beaks carefully after a feed. If you allow food to accumulate here, it may cause the beak to

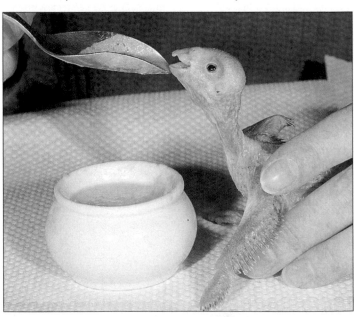

grow in a distorted fashion.

It is important that young chicks are kept warm. You can make a temporary brooder quite easily using light bulbs to heat a ventilated wooden box. Include a thermostat in the system, so that you can regulate the temperature, adjusting it as the chicks grow older. At first, they will need to be kept at incubation temperature, that is 37°C(99°F). Red or blue light bulbs are preferable, since these are less bright than the usual incandescent bulbs. The chicks themselves can be easily accommodated in empty, clean margarine pots or similar containers, lined with paper towelling. You will need to change this lining at each feed and, as the chicks grow older, you must enlarge their accommodation.

Brooder cages with low perches are ideal for chicks that are starting to feather up. Even though you will need to continue feeding the young parakeets by hand, you should introduce them to seed at this age. They will start pecking about on the base of the cage quite readily, and you will have to change the floor covering twice daily. From this stage onwards, provide drinking water in a closed vessel attached to the side of the cage.

Once you are certain that the parakeets are feeding independently, you can transfer them to the aviary. Never mix young birds with adults at this stage, however. Although not really delicate, recently fledged parakeets that have been reared by hand will need time to become established in their quarters, and you will obviously need to wait until the weather is fine before moving them to an outside aviary.

Caring for chicks in the aviary
Offer the widest possible range of foods to parent birds that are rearing their own chicks. Soaked millet sprays and greenfood, such as chickweed, are very popular with many Australian species, although pairs do show their own preferences. Check on the

progress of the chicks at intervals, but always avoid disturbing the nest when the hen is present.

As the time for fledging approaches, keep a close watch on the chicks of Australian species in case a cock bird becomes aggressive towards the chicks. Feather-plucking, although usually rare in parakeets, can be an indication that the chicks are being encouraged to leave the nest. The cock may also pursue the hen avidly at this time, and it is worthwhile providing a second nestbox in the flight for her. (Obviously, try to avoid any unnecessary disturbance when fixing it in place.)

A short time before the chicks are ready to fledge, the hen may lay a second clutch of eggs. Her mate will continue feeding the first clutch of chicks until a short time after they fledge. You should remove these chicks from the nest to another aviary or inside flight as soon as possible after fledging, even though this will create a disturbance if the hen has laid a second clutch. Leaving the hen in the flight, try to catch the chicks in the shelter. This will cause less upset and avoid the risk of the chicks flying hard into the mesh, and injuring themselves. This is a problem particularly prevalent with young Australian parakeets. Alternatively, if you have screened the far end of the flight with conifers or climbing plants, the fledglings will recognize this as a barrier.

Not all parakeets will nest twice in succession. Most psittaculid species, for example, will only rear one clutch in a season. However, if the first clutch of eggs fails to hatch, or if the chicks die at a very early age, there is every possibility that the hen will lay again. The onset of the moult usually marks the end of the breeding period. At this stage, you will need to decide which chicks to keep for the future. You can usually arrange to sell surplus stock or exchange the birds for new blood by advertising in the birdkeeping magazines, or contacting club members.

Parakeet genetics

Colour mutations in parakeets have largely been restricted to the Ring-necked Parakeet, but during recent years, many more mutations have emerged in Australian species and it is likely that these will become more widely available in the future. The fact that these parakeets will mature much earlier than the Ringnecks also means that the mutations will become established more quickly.

The transfer of colour and other features from one generation to the next is controlled by genes, which are present in the nucleus of every cell in the body, on paired structures called chromosomes. When mating takes place, the chromosomes from both parents randomly realign with each other. As a result, chicks receive one set of chromosomes, and thus genes, from each adult.

Some genes are dominant to others and will be expressed in the individual's appearance – its colour, for example – while the recessive character remains hidden. Only by selective pairings will recessive traits become apparent. In terms of genetic shorthand, the dominant character is written first, with an oblique line separating it from the recessive character, to denote that the bird is considered 'split' for the recessive feature (for example, normal/yellow).

Because they appear visually identical, you can only distinguish normals and 'splits' by trial pairings. Most mutations are, of course, recessive by nature, otherwise they would replace the normal form.

Autosomal recessive mutations
Most of the mutations are carried on the 'autosomes' – the name given to all chromosomes except the pair of chromosomes that determine the sex of the individual. Yellow, blue, and some pied mutations typically fall into this category. The five possible pairings of the normal with the yellow form of the Turquoisine Grass Parakeet are shown on the right.

It is important to remember that, because the chromosomes combine at random, the percentages given are averages, and are therefore unlikely to apply in every case. It is rather like tossing a coin and calling 'heads' or 'tails': the more times that you spin the coin, the nearer the average result will move towards 50% heads and 50% tails.

Below: *Colour mutations are now widely established in grass parakeets. This is a rosa Bourke.*

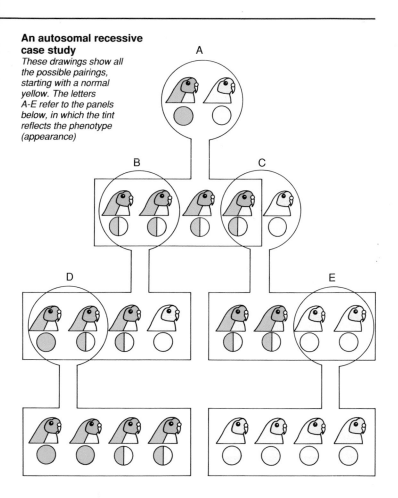

An autosomal recessive case study

These drawings show all the possible pairings, starting with a normal yellow. The letters A-E refer to the panels below, in which the tint reflects the phenotype (appearance)

A	Normal	x	yellow	→	100% normal/yellow		
B	Normal/ yellow	x	normal/ yellow	→	50% normal/ yellow	25% normal	25% yellow
C	Normal/ yellow	x	yellow	→	50% normal/ yellow	50% yellow	
D	Normal	x	normal/ yellow	→	50% normal	50% normal/ yellow	
E	Yellow	x	yellow	→	100% yellow		

Sex-linked recessive mutations

Here, the genes that determine the colour mutation occur on the sex chromosomes, which are the pair of chromosomes that determine the bird's gender. In the cock parakeet, these chromosomes are of equal length, but in the hen, one member of the pair is shorter in length. This means that the genes for the characteristic concerned remain unpaired, and so, in this instance alone, the bird's appearance must be a true reflection of its genetic make-up. The five possible pairings of the rosa form of the Bourke's Parakeet with the normal are shown in the chart on the right.

These results clearly show that it is better to purchase a cock of a sex-linked mutation and pair it with a normal hen, than vice versa. You will then be sure to obtain a proportion of sex-linked mutant offspring in the first generation. Furthermore, you can guarantee the sex of the offspring, and their genetic make-up, since all hens will be of the sex-linked colour, and all the cocks will be split.

Most cinnamon and lutino forms are sex-linked recessive mutations, with the notable exception of the rare lutino form of the Elegant Grass Parakeet, which is said to be of the autosomal recessive type. There is always the possibility, of course, that separate mutations of the same colour could arise. Both sex-linked and autosomal recessive forms of the lutino Ring-necked Parakeet have been recognized but as the latter now appears to be extinct, you can expect the lutinos to fall into the sex-linked category.

If you are in doubt as to whether a mutation is autosomal or sex-linked recessive, you can check the mode of inheritance by following the first pairing on the chart shown right. In the case of an autosomal recessive mutation, no first generation mutant offspring should result. However, you must be certain that the hen is not split for the mutation, otherwise this trial pairing will be invalid. Remember, too, that because of the random

A sex-linked recessive case study

Rosa cock	x	normal hen
Normal cock	x	rosa hen
Normal/ rosa cock	x	normal hen
Normal/ rosa cock	x	rosa hen
Rosa cock	x	rosa hen

A dominant case study

Grey-green (df)	x	green
Grey-green (sf)	x	green
Grey-green (sf)	x	grey-green (sf)
Grey-green (df)	x	grey-green (df)
Grey-green (df)	x	grey-green (sf)

way in which chromosomes combine, you should avoid making a judgement on the basis of one round of chicks. It is possible that all the offspring could be 'normals', although with a sex-linked mutation they would actually be split for the lutino characteristic.

Dominant mutations

Dominant mutations are exceedingly rare in parakeets, and the only confirmed example is the

→	50% normal/rosa cocks		50% rosa hens	
→	50% normal/rosa cocks		50% normal hens	
→	25% normal cocks	25% normal rosa cocks	25% normal hens	25% rosa hens
→	25% normal rosa cocks	25% rosa cocks	25% normal hens	25% rosa hens
→	50% rosa cocks		50% rosa hens	

→	100% grey-green (sf)		
→	50% grey-green (sf)	50% green	
→	50% grey-green (sf)	25% grey-green (df)	25% green
→	100% grey-green (df)		
→	50% grey-green (df)	50% grey-green (sf)	

grey mutation of the Ring-necked Parakeet. Such birds may be either double factor (df), if both chromosomes are affected, or single factor (sf), when only one chromosome is altered by the mutation. Here, we show the anticipated results of pairing a grey-green with a normal green Ring-necked Parakeet.

Again, it is impossible to distinguish between the single and double factor birds. However, in the Turquoisine Grass Parakeet species, a variant dominant mutation is known. This is the olive form, which is often described as an incomplete dominant mutation because of the difference in colour between the double factor and the single factor birds. The double factor is the olive form, whereas the single factor form, which is intermediate in colour between the olive and the normal, is described as the dark green.

Amboina King Parakeet
Alisterus amboinensis

● **Distribution**: From the Sula Islands to western New Guinea.
● **Size**: 36cm(14in).
● **Sexing**: Males tend to have red upper beaks, whereas those of hens are tinged with black markings.
● **Youngsters**: Distinguishable from adults by their green mantles and dark brown irides.

These spectacular parakeets are not common in European or North American collections, although the closely related Australian King Parakeet (*A. scapularis*) is quite widely kept in its native country. A third species, the Green-winged King Parakeet (*A. chloropterus*) may be seen occasionally, but, like other king parakeets, is expensive.

Differences in markings of Amboina King Parakeets result from their island distribution; six races are recognized by taxonomists.

King parakeets show to best effect in a long flight. Compatible pairs will nest satisfactorily, although sometimes cock birds can behave very aggressively towards their intended mates. The typical clutch of up to five eggs is incubated by the hen alone for about three weeks and the chicks fledge at two months old.

If you have the opportunity to purchase recently imported stock, remember that these birds need careful acclimatization.

Below: **Australian King Parakeet**
This species is easy to sex; cocks have red heads, whereas those of hens are green. A deep nestbox encourages breeding activity.

Crimson-winged Parakeet

Aprosmictus erythropterus

● **Distribution**: Northeastern and northern Australia, and southern New Guinea.
● **Size**: 33cm(13in).
● **Sexing**: Hens are duller than cocks, with no black mantle and a smaller area of red on the wings.
● **Youngsters**: Resemble hens, but have a yellowish bill at fledging.

This species, also known as the Red-winged Parakeet, prefers a deep nestbox. You can build this as a free-standing structure but as an

added precaution, you may decide to bolt it to the side of the aviary. Some cocks are aggressive and, if possible, you should make up pairs before the birds reach maturity, by three years of age. These parakeets prove reliable breeders; one pair on record produced 26 chicks over a nine-year period. Other breeding details are similar to those of the king parakeets, although youngsters may fledge at a slightly earlier age. They can live for over twenty years.

In the past, imported Crimson-wings have been badly infested with tapeworms, so it is advisable to administer appropriate treatment to newly purchased birds.

Another species of Crimsonwing, the Timor form, is found on some of the Lesser Sunda Islands but is rarely seen in avicultural collections at present.

Left: *The spectacular markings of the Crimson-winged Parakeet can be clearly seen here. Hens are less colourful than this cock.*

Below: **Crimson-winged Parakeet**
These parakeets may live for 20 years, and have a correspondingly long reproductive life.

Barnard's Parakeet
Barnardius barnardi

● **Distribution**: Interior parts of eastern Australia.
● **Size**: 33cm(13in).
● **Sexing**: Cocks generally have more colourful plumage than hens, particularly on their backs and abdomens.
● **Youngsters**: The crown and the nape of the neck are brownish.

The two members of this genus tend to rank amongst the least common and more expensive of the Australian parakeets in aviculture. Three separate races of Barnard's Parakeet are recognized. The Cloncurry (*B. b. macgillivrayi*) is the one you are most likely to encounter and this is also the most colourful form, with a prominent area of yellow plumage present on its underparts. Discovered as recently as 1900, this race occurs as an isolated population, found in northwestern Queensland and an adjoining part of the Northern Territory. It remains most common in continental Europe. Pairs have double-brooded (that is, bred twice in a season), producing as many as nine youngsters.

Below: **Barnard's Parakeet**
A cock may prove aggressive if you venture too close to its nestbox. Mealworms are popular with these birds during the rearing period.

Port Lincoln Parakeet
Barnardius zonarius

● **Distribution:** Over a wide area of western and central Australia.
● **Size:** 38cm(15in).
● **Sexing:** Hens usually have a more brownish head than cocks.
● **Youngsters:** Duller in colour than adults.

Both races of this species have become more common in aviculture during recent years, although they remain relatively expensive. The Twenty-eight Parakeet (*B. z. semitorquatus*) can be easily distinguished from the nominate race by its green rather than yellow abdomen and the red band usually present above the beak, surrounding the cere. Blue mutations of both have been recorded in the past and are said to be represented in European collections at the present time, although they are scarce.

As with Barnard's Parakeet, the incubation period lasts approximately 19 days, and the chicks fledge at around five weeks old. A few cocks are egg-eaters, and so you may need to remove cocks from the aviary as soon mating has taken place.

Below: **Port Lincoln Parakeet**
Like other Australian parakeets, these birds will often feed on the ground, so keep the floor clean.

Sierra Parakeet
Bolborhynchus aymara

● **Distribution:** Eastern Andes, from Bolivia to northwestern Argentina.
● **Size:** 20cm(8in).
● **Sexing**: It is generally difficult to distinguish between the sexes, but some cocks have dark grey heads and more silvery breasts.
● **Youngsters:** Similar to adults, but with shorter tails.

You may also find these delightful parakeets advertised under a variety of other names, such as the Aymara or the Andean Parakeet. They were first brought to Europe by Gerald Durrell, the famous naturalist, in 1959. Since then, there have been a number of further importations, but stock is now scarce. Nevertheless, they are prolific birds – they may rear up to seven chicks in one nest, and can be bred satisfactorily in groups. At present, however, reasonably large numbers are produced only by Danish breeders. Like other members of its genus, the Sierra Parakeet is quiet, with a high-pitched and not unattractive call. A further advantage of this species is that it is not very destructive.

Below: **Sierra Parakeets**
Sierra Parakeets breed well in the aviary and will use a conventional nestbox. (In the wild, they may nest in holes in prickly cacti, where they are out of reach of predators.)

Golden-fronted Parakeet
Bolborhynchus aurifrons

● **Distribution:** In isolated populations along the eastern side of South America, from Peru southwards to Chile.
● **Size:** 18cm(7in).
● **Sexing**: In some cases, males are more colourful than females.
● **Youngsters:** Similar to the hen.

Four separate populations of this parakeet have given rise to an equivalent number of races, so that birds purchased from different sources could turn out to be different sub-species.

Although doubts have been expressed about how well these parakeets travel, the few recent importations have had a very low level of mortality. Golden-fronted Parakeets do require a reasonable acclimatization period, but they are not delicate birds, and their poor survival rate in the past is more likely to have been caused by an unsuitable diet than by stress. Ensure that they receive a mixed diet of smaller cereal seeds, including millet sprays, greenfood, and regular supplies of fruit, such as apple and blackberries in season. Avoid excessive amounts of sunflower seeds.

Below: **Golden-fronted Parakeet**
These parakeets are variable in coloration; some cocks are more yellow than the one shown here.

Lineolated Parakeet
Bolborhynchus lineola

● **Distribution:** Central and South America, ranging from Mexico to Panama and from western Venezuela to central Peru.
● **Size:** 16cm(6in).
● **Sexing:** The barring on the rump and tail feathers is more prominent on cocks than on hens. These markings have given rise to its other name of Barred Parakeet.
● **Youngsters**: The bluish tinge on their heads is usually more pronounced than on adults.

This species is probably the most commonly available member of its genus in the UK at present. Its habits do not differ markedly from those of related parakeets.

Breeding on the colony system is quite feasible; indeed, you are likely to achieve better results if you can keep these birds in a group, rather than as individual pairs. Incubation lasts about 18 days and the chicks fledge at about five weeks old. The average clutch size varies from three to six eggs.

Below: **Lineolated Parakeet**
Quiet, attractive and free-breeding when kept in small groups, these birds are also less destructive than most parakeets. They appear to dislike very hot weather.

Right: **Cobalt-winged Parakeet**
These lively parakeets must have natural wood perches to gnaw in order to prevent their beaks becoming overgrown like this.

Cobalt-winged Parakeet
Brotogeris cyanoptera

● **Distribution:** Western Amazonian region, including parts of Colombia, Venezuela, Peru, Ecuador and Bolivia.
● **Size:** 18cm(7in).
● **Sexing:** Not visually possible.
● **Youngsters:** Duller overall in colour than adults, with a dark grey, rather than brown, upper mandible.

This is presently one of the less common members of the genus in avicultural circles. It can be distinguished from similar species by its violet-blue wing colour.

House these parakeets, and other *Brotogeris* species, in small groups if you want to breed them successfully. To minimize the risk of aggressive behaviour, position the nestboxes at the same height.

You may encounter problems if you have to remove one member from an established group of Cobaltwings; it will lose its place in the flock hierarchy, and when you try to return it, even just a few days later, it will be treated as a newcomer, and may be attacked. Ideally, if you do need to remove or add one bird, you should transfer all the parakeets to temporary accommodation for up to a week, before reintroducing them all to the original flight. They should then accept one another more readily. Do not mix different *Brotogeris* species together, however, as hybridization can occur.

Tovi Parakeet
Brotogeris jugularis

● **Distribution:** Southwestern parts of Mexico, and northern parts of Colombia and Venezuela.
● **Size:** 18cm(7cm).
● **Sexing:** Not visually possible.
● **Youngsters:** Resemble adults.

This is another species that is known under a variety of common names, including Bee-Bee Parrot and, more accurately, the Orange-chinned Parakeet. This characteristic and the dark, olive-brown wing markings of these parakeets are both identifying features. In the wild, Tovis remain in flocks at all times of the year and may use the nests of termites, located in trees. In captivity, significant breeding results have been obtained only when these parakeets have been housed in colonies. As many as eight young have been reared by a single pair, and are mature at one year old.

Below: **Tovi Parakeet**
Like all Brotogeris *parakeets, Tovis nest more readily if they are kept together as a group, and are hardy once acclimatized.*

Grey-cheeked Parakeet
Brotogeris pyrrhopterus

● **Distribution:** South America, in coastal areas of western Ecuador and northwestern Peru.
● **Size:** 20cm(8in).
● **Sexing:** Not visually possible.
● **Youngsters:** Their green heads lack the bluish markings of adults.

These birds, also called Orange-flanked or Orange-winged Parakeets because of the prominent orange area on the undersides of the wings, used to be freely available but are now scarce. Like all *Brotogeris*, tame youngsters were once very popular pets, but few were kept by serious breeders. They have quite a loud call, which can become persistent if the parakeet is upset. Youngsters often form a strong bond with their owners, and may become jealous of other pets. Assorted fruits need to form a significant part of the diet of this group of parakeets. Banana is a favourite food, although it can be messy, sticking to perches and the sides of the cage, and sweet apple is also very popular. You can also feed soaked dried fruits occasionally, and drained canned fruits, preferably those that have been mixed with natural juice rather than syrup, are also suitable.

Below: **Grey-cheeked Parakeet**
Also known as the Orange-flanked Parakeet because of the colourful orange plumage hidden under its wings, this bird is highly gregarious by nature and can be destructive.

Canary-winged Parakeet
Brotogeris versicolorus

● **Distribution:** Over a wide area of the Amazon Basin, and further south, across Brazil, to Bolivia, Paraguay and Argentina.
● **Size:** 23cm(9in).
● **Sexing:** Not visually possible.
● **Youngsters:** Usually duller in colour than adults.

Two very distinct forms of this parakeet are recognized: the White-winged race (*B. v. versicolorus*) is much darker in colour and has paler yellow wing markings than the Canary-winged, which has been the most commonly available member of the genus for many years.

Once acclimatized, these parakeets are quite hardy, but you should encourage them to roost in the shelter if they will not use a nestbox. Records of successful breeding are scarce, but four eggs appear to form the typical clutch, and these hatch after about 26 days. The chicks fledge at approximately seven weeks old.

Below: **Canary-winged Parakeets**
Young birds can develop into very tame pets. Fruit is a favourite of these and all Brotogeris *species. Offer some every day.*

Yellow-fronted Kakariki
Cyanoramphus auriceps

● **Distribution:** New Zealand and neighbouring islands.
● **Size:** 23cm(9in).
● **Sexing:** Males are larger than females, with bolder coloration.
● **Youngsters:** Recognizable by their shorter tails and brown irides.

This species is slightly smaller than the better-known Red-fronted Kakariki. The unusual name of these parakeets is said to describe their call, and originates from a Maori word. They make ideal occupants for a garden aviary, as they are quiet and usually keen to breed. Pairs normally nest twice in a season, laying between five and nine eggs, which hatch after a period of 19 days. The hen will usually lay again before her first chicks have left the nest, at about six weeks old, and the cock will then feed them for a few more days until they are able to eat on their own. You should then remove the young birds before the cock becomes aggressive towards them.

Below: **Yellow-fronted Kakariki**
These New Zealand parakeets are becoming increasingly popular. Pairs nest readily and mature quickly, but avoid breeding birds that are less than a year old.

Left: *An example of the very scarce yellow mutation of the Yellow-fronted Kakariki.*

Red-fronted Kakariki
Cyanoramphus novaezelandiae

● **Distribution:** New Zealand and neighbouring islands.
● **Size:** 28cm(11in).
● **Sexing:** Hens are usually slightly smaller than cocks.
● **Youngsters:** The area of red on the head is smaller, and the tail shorter than that of adults.

Both these species of kakariki are unusual aviary birds, scratching around on the floor with their feet, and capable of running straight up the mesh to a perch without using their beaks. If you have adjoining aviaries, it is therefore vital that you install double-wiring to protect them from other parakeets in neighbouring flights (see page 28).

Kakarikis will benefit from a very varied diet, which can include softbill food and livefood, such as mealworms. They also enjoy greenfood and various berries.

Mutations have been recorded in these prolific birds, including a lutino and a pied form, which is at present being developed in the UK.

Above: **Red-fronted Kakariki**
This is a prolific and popular aviary species but has a maximum lifespan of about five years.

Top: *The distinctive head markings of the Red-fronted Kakariki. Young birds have brown eyes and are less colourful than this adult.*

Quaker Parakeet
Myiopsitta monachus

● **Distribution:** Bolivia and parts of Brazil and Argentina.
● **Size:** 29cm(11.5in).
● **Sexing:** Not visually possible.
● **Youngsters:** Recognizable by the green tinge to their foreheads.

The breeding habits of these interesting but rather noisy parakeets are unique. Although they will use a nestbox, they often prefer to build a nest of twigs in the aviary, as they do in the wild. These nests can become very large and will be difficult to look into, which is a disadvantage. If you do decide to try this method of breeding, therefore, provide the birds with a stout horizontal mesh support, fixed onto the side of the flight, and a supply of twigs. (Even in a nestbox, Quakers will include pieces of wood taken from perches if they do not have access to twigs.) You are likely to obtain the best results by keeping these birds in a colony. Up to seven eggs form the usual clutch.

Colour mutations are known, the blue form being the most common. It is usual to pair a blue with a normal because of a lethal factor, which prevents some of the embryos from hatching if two blues are paired together. A rarer yellow mutant has also been bred.

Below: **Quaker Parakeet**
These fascinating birds live in colonies in the wild and build large, bulky nests of sticks.

67

Bourke's Grass Parakeet

Neophema bourkii

● **Distribution:** The interior of southern and central Australia.
● **Size:** 19cm(7.5in).
● **Sexing:** Hens have a mainly white forehead, whereas that of males is entirely blue.
● **Youngsters:** Resemble hens, but have paler pink abdomens. Young hens have a well-developed wing stripe.

These highly popular parakeets are the only grass parakeets that show no green coloration in their plumage. Their eyes are relatively large, confirming that they become more active towards dusk.

Pairs will usually breed readily in aviary surroundings, with the hen laying up to five eggs. She incubates these alone for about 19 days, and the chicks leave the nest for the first time when they are just over a month old. Once they

Above: **Bourke's Grass Parakeet**
This small attractive parakeet is widely available. Pairs will often nest twice during the summer.

Below: *This is the yellow rosa form of the Bourke's Grass Parakeet. A number of such colour mutations have now been developed.*

become independent, shortly after this, you should remove them so that the adult pair can continue breeding without interference.

During recent years, the rosa mutation, also known in continental Europe as the opaline, has become quite common. The effect of this mutation is to increase and intensify the soft reddish coloration most noticeable on the belly of the normal-coloured bird. You can distinguish young Bourke's of this form from normals while they are still in the nest; by ten days of age, the feet of normals have darkened in colour, whereas rosa Bourke's retain pinkish feet throughout their lives. Other rarer mutations include a yellow, which has a pinkish head and breast, and a cinnamon. Apart from its reddish eyes, this cinnamon form closely resembles a normal in appearance.

Above: *The dark, blackish markings of the normal form of the Bourke's Grass Parakeet are modified to a paler shade of brown in the cinnamon, shown here.*

Left: *This rosa form of the Bourke's Grass Parakeet is the most colourful and widely kept mutation by virtue of its strong pink coloration. Hens have paler faces.*

Blue-winged Grass Parakeet

Neophema chrysostomus

● **Distribution:** Southeastern Australia, including Tasmania.
● **Size:** 20cm(8in).
● **Sexing:** Hens have olive-green crowns and duller blue wings, whereas cocks are more colourful, with black, rather than brownish black, primary flight feathers.
● **Youngsters:** Wing stripes are always present in young hens, but not always in cocks. Juveniles of both sexes lack the blue frontal band of adult birds.

This species has never achieved the popularity of other grass

Above:
Blue-winged Grass Parakeet
This species is less common than other grass parakeets, but is as easy to care for as its relatives.

parakeets, possibly because it is less colourful. In its favour, it lays its first clutch of eggs slightly later in the year than other parakeets so that the likelihood of egg-binding is greatly reduced. Bluewings can be prolific breeders and often double-brood; one pair are on record as having produced 68 chicks to fledging over a nine-year period. A further advantage of Blue-winged Grass Parakeets is that the fledglings are rarely as nervous as those of other related species.

Elegant Grass Parakeet
Neophema elegans

● **Distribution:** South-west and south-east Australia.
● **Size:** 23cm(9in).
● **Sexing**: Hens tend to be duller in colour than the cocks, without any orange visible on the abdomen.
● **Youngsters:** Similar to hens, but lacking the frontal band.

These parakeets are well established in aviculture and will nest readily in the aviary. Breeding details are similar to those of Bourke's Parakeet (and some other members of the genus).

A beautiful, bright yellow lutino form, with red eyes and white head and wing markings, was produced in Belgium during the 1970s. The loss of surrounding pigment emphasizes the orange between the legs of cock birds of this mutation. Unfortunately, the first chick died at a few months old, and the strain proved to have poor fertility. Interestingly, this is one of the very few lutino mutations known in parrots to be of the autosomal recessive form, rather than having a sex-linked mode of inheritance (see *Parakeet genetics,* page 50). Cinnamon and pied forms are also being developed.

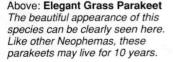

Above: **Elegant Grass Parakeet**
The beautiful appearance of this species can be clearly seen here. Like other Neophemas, these parakeets may live for 10 years.

Above: This rare lutino form of the Elegant Grass Parakeet was first bred during 1972 in Belgium. Initially the strain was weak, but such birds are now much stronger.

71

Turquoisine Grass Parakeet

Neophema pulchella

● **Distribution:** Southeastern Australia.
● **Size:** 20cm(8in).
● **Sexing:** Hens are duller than cocks, and lack the red wing patches of the latter.
● **Youngsters**: Similar to hens. A slight outline of the wing patches may be visible on young cocks.

The Turquoisine Parakeet is a very common species in aviculture, but its status in the wild is unclear and it may be becoming increasingly rare in its natural habitat. There is an orange-bellied form of the Turquoisine, which is very popular, and birds with this distinctive coloration are known to occur in the wild. Among the mutations bred in collections are yellow, pied and olive forms. The pied mutation of this parakeet is a sex-linked recessive character, rather than the autosomal recessive type (see *Parakeet genetics*, page 50).

As aviary subjects, these parakeets are rather more aggressive than related species. If possible, avoid keeping pairs in adjoining aviaries, since cocks, especially, will bicker through the mesh. They will also attack their youngsters soon after fledging. Young Turquoisines are probably the most nervous of all the grass parakeets. Screening the end of the flight with climbing plants, such as nasturtiums, may help to reduce the risk of injuries.

Below:
Turquoisine Grass Parakeet
A colourful and popular species. Hens lack the distinctive deep red wing patches of this cock bird.

Right: *Two mutations of the Turquoisine Grass Parakeet. A red-fronted cock and yellow hen.*

Above: *It has proved possible to combine various mutations of the Turquoisine. These parakeets, the result of combining the red-bellied form with the yellow mutation, are strikingly colourful birds.*

Right: *These orange-bellied Turquoisines are identical to the more common yellow-bellied form, apart from the coloration of their belly. Birds of this colour have been reported in the wild.*

Splendid Parakeet
Neophema splendida

● **Distribution:** The interior of southern Australia.
● **Size:** 19cm(7.5in).
● **Sexing:** Cocks are instantly recognized by their scarlet chests.
● **Youngsters:** Similar to hens, but cocks may have bluer faces. Young cocks start to show red feathers on their breasts from about two months after fledging.

These stunningly beautiful parakeets used to be very scarce, but aviary stock is now well established. This species provides an excellent introduction to the hobby of breeding parakeets, since pairs are relatively inexpensive and usually become quite tame in aviary surroundings.

Several mutations have been bred, of which the most common is currently the blue form. However, as with the Quaker Parakeet (see page 60), blue stock should not be paired together because of the lethal factor. These particular birds are not pure blue in coloration, but have a greenish tinge to their plumage. Yellow, cinnamon and fallow forms are also recognized.

Below: **Splendid Parakeet**
This beautiful species has proved extremely prolific in aviaries.

Right: *The cinnamon mutation of the Splendid Parakeet. This is a hen bird, lacking the bright chest marking of the cock. Such birds are somewhat paler than the normals.*

Below: *The blue mutation of the Splendid Parakeet. This is not a pure blue; the outline of the red breast of the normal cock is still visible as a pale shade of orange.*

Mealy Rosella
Platycercus adscitus

● **Distribution:** Northeastern Australia.
● **Size:** 30cm(12in).
● **Sexing:** Cocks lack the wing stripe of hens.
● **Youngsters:** Duller in coloration than the hen, juveniles may also have red or grey markings on their heads.

The rosellas, or broadtails, as they are otherwise known, are a group of eight Australian species, which are generally well represented in aviculture. There are two distinctive

Above: **Mealy Rosella**
These attractive rosellas are larger than the grass parakeets, and need more spacious aviaries. Mealies are lively by nature.

sub-species of this particular rosella in the wild; the nominate race is the Blue-cheeked (*P. a. adscitus*), while the Mealy itself (*P. a. palliceps*) has pure white, rather than blue, feathering surrounding the lower beak. Unfortunately, indiscriminate pairings in the past have obscured these features in aviary-bred stock, although well-marked Mealy Rosellas can occasionally be seen.

77

Green Rosella
Platycercus caledonicus

● **Distribution:** Tasmania and some neighbouring islands.
● **Size:** 36cm(14in).
● **Sexing:** Hens tend to be smaller than cocks and may have orange-red markings on the throat.
● **Youngsters:** Duller in colour than adults with blue cheek patches and a wing stripe.

These parakeets, sometimes also known as Tasmanian Rosellas, have tended to be less popular than their more colourful counterparts, although increasing numbers are being bred in European collections.

These rosellas eat greenfood eagerly; if possible, provide fresh supplies each day, but remember that excessive amounts may lead to scouring. A standard seed diet, comprised of cereals with some sunflower and pine nuts, suits all rosellas well and they may also take fruit in their diet.

A related species, the Yellow Rosella (*P. flaveolus*), shown below, is similar in appearance and requirements to the Green Rosella, but is relatively uncommon.

Below: **Yellow Rosella**
This species is often confused with its relative, the Green Rosella, but is slightly smaller, more brightly coloured, and rarer.

Crimson Rosella
Platycercus elegans

● **Distribution:** Eastern and southeastern parts of Australia.
● **Size:** 36cm(14in).
● **Sexing:** Visual sexing is difficult, although hens may have smaller heads than cocks.
● **Youngsters:** Juveniles vary in appearance; some are mainly green, whereas others are predominantly reddish, more closely resembling adults.

Below: **Crimson Rosella**
Among the most striking and popular of all rosellas, these birds can prove very prolific breeders in aviary surroundings.

Also known as Pennant's Parakeet, this is one of the most widely kept rosellas, and a blue mutation is also now established. Although hardy and easy to keep, some individuals are prone to feather-plucking and will pull out their feathers until their body is covered only in grey down. This is a difficult problem to overcome, but such birds will breed normally.

Established pairs can be very prolific, rearing as many as seven chicks or more, although some hens will eat the eggs or refuse to incubate properly. As a consequence, it is best to start with young birds, rather than attempt to breed adults, which may have these vices. The birds will be mature by one year old.

Rosellas will hybridize with each other and, in the wild, this tendency appears to have given rise to the Adelaide Rosella. This population is thought to result from Crimson and Yellow Rosellas breeding together in two small areas of Southern Australia. Trial matings in aviary surroundings have confirmed the appearance of such offspring and, unusually, these hybrids are themselves fertile.

Below: **Adelaide Rosella**
This species could be a natural hybrid, resulting from matings of Crimson and Yellow Rosellas.

Eastern Rosella
Platycercus eximius

● **Distribution:** Southeastern Australia and Tasmania.
● **Size:** 30cm(12in).
● **Sexing:** Hens are duller than cocks, with a reduced area of red on the head and breast.
● **Youngsters:** Distinguishable by their green napes and hind crown.

These rosellas usually prove reliable breeders, laying on average six or seven eggs. As with other species, the incubation period lasts about three weeks. Chicks leave the nest when approximately six weeks old, and can breed during their second year, before they have moulted into full adult plumage. (This normally occurs by the age of fifteen months.) All rosellas have a potentially long lifespan and are quite capable of breeding into their twenties.

Below: **Eastern Rosellas**
These parakeets, often known as Golden-mantled Rosellas, are very popular as aviary birds.

Above: *The rare pastel mutation of the Eastern Rosella shows the characteristic paling of the normal form's dark markings.*

Western Rosella
Platycercus icterotis

● **Distribution:** Southwestern Australia.
● **Size:** 25cm(10in).
● **Sexing:** Clearly dimorphic, hens are much duller than cocks, with a greenish head and underparts.
● **Youngsters:** Almost entirely green at fledging.

This species, which is perhaps more often called the Stanley Parakeet, is the smallest member of the *Platycercus* genus.

Western Rosellas are less common, and consequently more costly, than other rosellas. The reason is simply that they do not double-brood, rearing only one round of chicks each year. However, as a prolific pair can lay as many as eight eggs in a clutch, you may still be able to achieve good breeding results.

Colour mutations of this parakeet are unknown, and remain very rare in other rosellas, too.

Below: **Western Rosella**
Less common than its larger relatives, this species is easy to sex; the cock, shown here, with a red head and underparts, is more colourful than the hen.

Princess of Wales' Parakeet
Polytelis alexandrae

● **Distribution:** The interior of western and central Australia.
● **Size:** 45cm(18in).
● **Sexing:** Hens have greyish rather than light blue crowns, and a greyer rump than cocks.
● **Youngsters:** Similar to the hen.

The attractive pastel coloration of these parakeets has ensured their popularity, and they have been bred in increasing numbers during recent years. At least two colour mutations have appeared; the blue form was first bred in Australia in 1951 and, more recently, a lutino mutation was developed by an East German breeder in 1975.

One of the most desirable features of the Princess of Wales' Parakeet, besides its coloration, is the fact that it will become very tame in aviary surroundings with little persuasion. Unfortunately, the penetrating calls of adult birds may cause problems, particularly in an urban environment. Breeding details are similar to those of other members of the genus.

Below: *The blue mutation of the Princess of Wales' Parakeet is becoming increasingly common. This is an autosomal recessive mutation (see page 50).*

Below:
Princess of Wales' Parakeet
A few pairs may be egg-eaters.

Rock Pebbler (Peplar)
Polytelis anthopeplus

● **Distribution:** Southwestern Australia, and in an inland area of southeastern Australia.
● **Size:** 40cm(16in).
● **Sexing:** Hens, which are predominantly olive-yellow in colour, are much duller than cocks.
● **Youngsters**: Similar to hens.

These parakeets are also called Regent Parrots. Some pairs prefer to nest close to the ground, especially in flights containing ample vegetation. Do not encourage this behaviour, however, especially if the area is exposed to the elements. The red markings on the cock's wings feature prominently in its mating display. The hen lays about five eggs, which she incubates for about 19 days. The young parakeets will emerge into the aviary about six weeks later, but may not breed themselves until they are two years old.

Below: **Rock Pebbler**
Like other larger Australian species, youngsters usually start breeding during their second year.

Barraband Parakeet

Polytelis swainsonii

● **Distribution:** Interior of southeastern Australia.
● **Size:** 40cm(16in).
● **Sexing:** Hens can be easily recognized by the lack of yellow plumage on their heads.
● **Youngsters:** Resemble hens, but have dark brown irides.

This species, the third and final member of the *Polytelis* genus, is also known as the Superb Parrot. Like all the larger Australian species, this very majestic bird needs a long flight, both for its comfort, and for its beauty to be seen to advantage. These parakeets are quite gentle by nature and pairs do best when housed in close proximity to each other, as they are naturally social. It has even proved possible to breed more than one pair in a large aviary, although some cocks may be aggressive. Young males are still at risk from their paternal parent when they emerge from the nest, and so, as always, you should remove the chicks as soon as they are feeding independently.

Below: **Barraband Parakeet**
Note the distinctive yellow head of this adult cock. Immature males are recognizable by their song.

Red-rumped Parakeet
Psephotus haematonotus

● **Distribution:** Southeastern Australia.
● **Size:** 27cm(11in).
● **Sexing:** Cocks are far more colourful than the greyish green hens.
● **Youngsters:** Resemble adults, but young hens have yellower beaks than adults, while those of cocks are grey rather than black.

The Red-rumped Parakeet is by far the best-known member of its genus, of which five species are found in aviculture, and pairs make attractive aviary occupants. The

cocks have a very appealing musical song, but they can be savage, especially towards male offspring, which they may attack even while they are still in the nestbox. Five eggs form a typical clutch, and incubation lasts around 19 days. The chicks will be ready to leave the nest by the time they are six weeks old.

A dull yellow form has been developed and used to be the most commonly bred Australian parakeet mutation. A blue form, which emerged during 1968 in Australia, is presently being developed, along with a lutino mutation. In time, by careful pairings, it should be possible to produce an albino form using these two primary mutations.

Other members of this genus that you may occasionally encounter are the Many-coloured or Mulga Parakeet (*P. varius*), which tends to be somewhat more delicate than the hardy Redrump, and the Blue-bonnet Parakeet (*P. haematogaster*), of which Red- and Yellow-vented races are known.

Below: **Red-rumped Parakeets**
These popular parakeets are easy to sex and usually breed well.

Left: *The yellow mutation of the Red-rumped Parakeet. Hens are duller than this cock.*

Moustached Parakeet
Psittacula alexandri

● **Distribution:** From the Himalayas of northern India, eastwards across south-east Asia, to offshore islands, including Java and Bali.
● **Size:** 33cm(13in).
● **Sexing:** In most cases, hens can be recognized by their black beaks, whereas those of cocks are red.
● **Youngsters:** Duller overall in colour than adults, juveniles also have shorter tails.

The 12 species of psittaculid parakeet are found mainly in Asia and on a number of the offshore islands in this region. The Moustached Parakeet has a wide distribution, and up to eight different races can be identified over this area. Both sexes of the Javan sub-species (*P. a. alexandri*), have a reddish bill, but the distinctions are more marked between other races.

Moustached Parakeets are attractive, although rather noisy, birds. Once imported in large numbers, they are now quite scarce. Few breeding results have been recorded, but this would appear to be due largely to a lack of interest on the part of birdkeepers, rather than to intrinsic difficulties in persuading these birds to nest. Incubation normally lasts about 28 days, with two or three eggs forming the usual clutch. The young fledge when just over seven weeks old.

Below: **Moustached Parakeet**
An attractive species. Established pairs breed quite readily, but need to be carefully acclimatized first.

Plum-headed Parakeet
Psittacula cyanocephala

● **Distribution:** Sri Lanka and most of India.
● **Size:** 33cm(13in).
● **Sexing:** Adult cocks have plum-coloured heads, whereas those of hens are greyish.
● **Youngsters:** Resemble hens, although they initially fledge with green heads.

These highly attractive parakeets are ideal members of this genus to keep in an urbanized setting, since they are not noisy; indeed, their calls are actually quite melodious.

It can be difficult to obtain pairs, as a relatively high proportion of youngsters appear to moult out as cocks. The earliest traces of plum-coloured feathering can be seen close to the cere. Plumheads nest quite early in the year if allowed to do so, and unfortunately, they will stop brooding their chicks at an early stage, which can prove fatal. In cold climates, they will breed quite satisfactorily in an indoor flight, provided that you keep the temperature reasonably high. Like other psittaculids, they are at risk from frostbite, and need adequate protection during cold weather.

A similar parakeet, the Blossom-headed, occurs further east than the Plumhead. It is a slightly smaller form, and hens can be distinguished from Plumhead hens by their red wing patches. Most taxonomists now see these as being related sub-species.

Below: **Plum-headed Parakeet**
This is a mature cock. These birds are quieter and less destructive than other psittaculids.

Alexandrine Parakeet
Psittacula eupatria

● **Distribution:** From eastern Afghanistan through India to Indo-China. Also present in Sri Lanka.
● **Size:** 58cm(23in).
● **Sexing:** Adult hens lack the neck ring of cocks.
● **Youngsters:** Resemble hens, but have shorter tails.

These large, spectacular parakeets are mature, in most cases, during their third year and, once established, pairs will nest consistently for up to two decades. Two or three eggs form the usual clutch and should hatch after an incubation period of 28 days.

Young hand-reared Alexandrines can develop into lively, trusting companions, although they are not great mimics and may be destructive towards any exposed woodwork in their aviary. Pine nuts, peanuts and sweet apple are favoured food items. Never be tempted to buy an Alexandrine (or indeed a Ring-necked Parakeet) with a pink neck collar if you are seeking a youngster as such birds will be at least two years old.

Below: **Alexandrine Parakeet**
Genuine blue and lutino colour forms of this species are known, but matings with mutation Ringnecks have also been used to create such colours artificially.

Slaty headed Parakeet
Psittacula himalayana

● **Distribution:** In a band stretching from eastern Afghanistan to India and Nepal, southeastwards to Indo-china.
● **Size:** 40cm(16in).
● **Sexing:** Hens either lack the deep maroon wing patch of cocks, or it is only faintly visible.
● **Youngsters:** Recognizable by their green heads and cheeks.

The Slaty headed Parakeet is similar to, though less commonly available than, the Plum-headed Parakeet. Hybridization between

Above: **Slaty headed Parakeet**
Both sexes are characterized by their slaty grey head, but hens lack the cock's maroon wing patch, which is just visible here.

these two species has been reported, and in the wild may have given rise to the so-called Intermediate Parakeet (*P. intermedia*), which shares the characteristics of both species. This very rare Intermediate Parakeet is thought to occur in the region of Uttar Pradesh in India.

Up to five eggs appear to form the usual clutch, and these hatch after about 26 days.

Ring-necked Parakeet
Psittacula krameri

● **Distribution:** Occurs naturally across a wide belt of northern Africa, and also in India and adjoining areas.
● **Size:** 40cm(16in).
● **Sexing:** Hens lack the nuchal collars of cocks.
● **Youngsters:** Resemble hens, but have shorter tail feathers.

This is the most widely distributed of all parakeet species. The Indian race (*P. k. manillensis*) is slightly larger than the African (*P. k. krameri*), and the pink collar of the cock bird is often rather more pronounced on the former. The African Ringneck has a much darker beak, with black markings on the upper mandible. Both forms have been popular avicultural subjects for many years.

Ringnecks may occasionally breed when two years old, but it is usually three years before they are fully mature. In northern climates mating takes place early in the year

Below:
Indian Ring-necked Parakeet
Only mature cock birds have this neck collar. Juvenile males resemble adult hens.

and Ringnecks are often one of the first species to start nesting. The hen may lay up to six eggs and these will hatch after a period of about 24 days. The chicks fledge when they are around 50 days old and it is unusual, though not unknown, for the adults to nest again that season unless the first round of eggs fail to hatch or the chicks die at an early age.

Many colour mutations have been established, some of which, such as the blue, are known to have originated in the wild. The lutino is presently the most common mutation and when this is combined with the blue, pure albino Ringnecks, which lack any colour pigment and so have no neck collar, result. Other mutations include cinnamons, greys and a greenish blue form, sometimes called the Pastel Blue. Sometimes pied markings may be due to nutritional factors rather than of genetic origin, in which case they will disappear after a moult.

Above: *This stunning blue mutation of the Ring-necked Parakeet is becoming increasingly widespread.*

Below: *The lutino is now the most common mutation of the Ring-necked Parakeet. These two young lutino chicks are 16 weeks old.*

Above: *An albino Ring-necked Parakeet. With no colour pigment present, both sexes appear identical and can be distinguished only by surgical sexing.*

Right: *This grey form of the Indian Ringneck is usually a dominant mutation, although a paler recessive form is being developed in North America.*

Top: *The attractive head markings of the Long-tailed Parakeet are clearly visible here. Note the orange upper beak of this cock.*

Above: **Long-tailed Parakeet**
Regular spraying with tepid water will improve the feathering of such birds while kept indoors.

Long-tailed Parakeet
Psittacula longicauda

● **Distribution:** Malay peninsula, and offshore islands such as the Andamans, Borneo and Sumatra.
● **Size:** 42cm(17in).
● **Sexing:** Hens have brown upper beaks, whereas those of cocks are reddish in colour.
● **Youngsters:** Mainly green, with short tail feathers.

There are few of these attractive members of the psittaculid group in collections today. Long-tailed Parakeets originate from farther south than related species, and this may partly explain why they are so vulnerable to frostbite. Certainly, they need to be kept in warm accommodation over the winter months. Post-mortem studies have revealed that they are also prone to blood parasites, notably *microfilariae*, which can form knots in their circulatory system, with a fatal outcome. In view of their susceptibility to circulatory disease, including fatty deposits in their blood vessels, you should give them a low-fat diet and plenty of fruit. However, these are really parakeets for the dedicated specialist only.

Long-tailed Parakeets lay two or three eggs, which the hen incubates alone for about 25 days. The young fledge after approximately six weeks.

93

Index of species

Page numbers in **bold** indicate major references including accompanying photographs. Page numbers in *italics* indicate captions to other illustrations. Less important text entries are shown in normal type.